IMAGES
of America

SAN FRANCISCO'S
1939–1940 WORLD'S FAIR
THE GOLDEN GATE
INTERNATIONAL EXPOSITION

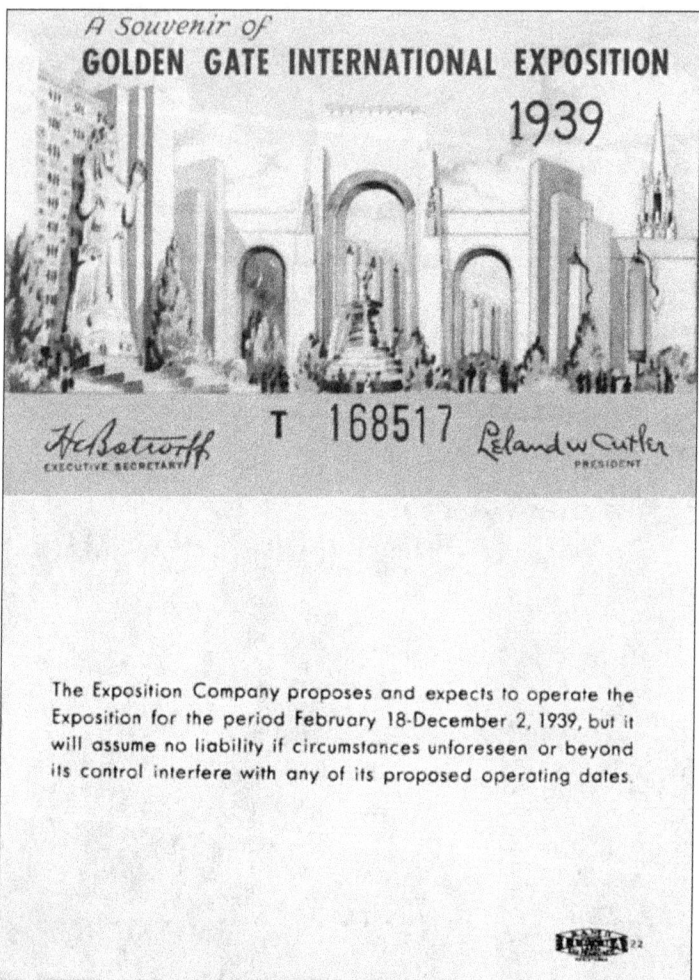

A Souvenir of

GOLDEN GATE INTERNATIONAL EXPOSITION

1939

H.C.Bottorff
EXECUTIVE SECRETARY

T 168517

Leland w Cutler
PRESIDENT

The Exposition Company proposes and expects to operate the Exposition for the period February 18-December 2, 1939, but it will assume no liability if circumstances unforeseen or beyond its control interfere with any of its proposed operating dates.

When the organizers of the Golden Gate International Exposition printed the tickets, they left themselves a legal loophole in case they had to close the gates earlier than the planned end date of December 2, 1939. As things turned out, it was a good thing they did. (Author's collection.)

ON THE COVER: The Tower of the Sun, the exposition's unofficial theme structure, stood at the center of the Court of Honor, near the main entrance. In the foreground, the fountain in the Treasure Garden soars into the sky. (Author's collection.)

IMAGES
of America

SAN FRANCISCO'S
1939–1940 WORLD'S FAIR
THE GOLDEN GATE
INTERNATIONAL EXPOSITION

Bill Cotter

ARCADIA
PUBLISHING

Published by Arcadia Publishing
Charleston, South Carolina

Library of Congress Control Number: 2020946131

For all general information, please contact Arcadia Publishing:
Telephone 843-853-2070
Fax 843-853-0044
E-mail sales@arcadiapublishing.com
For customer service and orders:
Toll-Free 1-888-313-2665

Visit us on the Internet at www.arcadiapublishing.com

*I am deeply indebted to my wife, Carol, for her ongoing
support and understanding of my desire to fill the house
with vintage photographs of events long past. Without her
assistance and encouragement, this book would not exist.*

CONTENTS

ACKNOWLEDGMENTS

Writing a book like this about an event as large as the Golden Gate International Exposition is always a collaborative effort. No matter how many pictures I have collected over the years, there will always be some images that have eluded me, or reference material that is not easily accessible. I have appreciated the help of others on my past books, but the forced closures of most reference facilities due to COVID-19 posed a unique set of challenges this time. Happily, a number of my fellow world's fair fans and enthusiasts stepped up and helped me finish the project. My thanks to Ralph Quinn, Laurent Antoine LeMog, Vince Bravo, and the San Francisco History Center at the San Francisco Public Library for the use of selected images as noted. All other images are from the author's collection.

Thanks also to Anne Schnoebelen, a volunteer at the Treasure Island Museum, for assistance on the research front. The museum was established in 1975 to preserve the island's history as a world's fair site, airport, and Navy base. It is located in the fair's former administration building; for more information, please visit www.treasureislandmuseum.org.

I am also indebted to Randy Lopes and my wife, Carol Cotter, for their proofreading and editing skills, which are greatly appreciated, and to a very patient editor, Angel Prohaska, for her understanding of the twists and turns in completing this book despite the unexpected obstacles that popped up along the way.

INTRODUCTION

Growing up in New York, I thought I knew all about the 1939 world's fair. It was the big event in Queens with the Trylon and Perisphere, and my parents and their friends talked about going to it. It was not until years later when I moved to California that I first heard there had been another fair at the same time, that one in San Francisco.

When I started researching this "other" fair, I was immediately fascinated. The Golden Gate International Exposition, as it was formally known, was an extremely ambitious project with a fascinating path to its creation. The affair began in 1933 when Joseph E. Dixon, a retired real estate businessman, suggested a world's fair be held to celebrate the planned completion of the new Golden Gate and Bay Bridges in 1937. Chicago had recently held a very popular fair in 1933–1934, and surely San Francisco could do the same. After all, it had already hosted the Panama-Pacific International Exposition of 1915 to great success.

Other cities had taken note of the Chicago fair and were also exploring the possibility of hosting such an event. Los Angeles was floating the idea for a "Pacific Exposition" in 1937 to commemorate the building of Boulder Dam, and in Oregon, the city of Portland looked to celebrate the completion of the Bonneville Dam with a gala in 1937 or 1938. Frustrated by his lack of success in igniting interest with local politicians and not wanting San Francisco to lose out to these competitors, Dixon eventually penned a letter to the *San Francisco News*. The paper published it, and public support exploded. Seeing the public mood, the politicians finally jumped onboard, and the San Francisco fair was underway.

Another major project was being studied at the same time, one that would intersect favorably with the fair's efforts. The city had long been looking to build a new airport to position itself as the premier base for air travel to the Pacific region. Ideally, it had to be on the waterfront as only seaplanes had the needed range, but all of the sites investigated were fully devoted to other uses. The fair team and the airport team eventually joined forces and came up with a unique solution—a man-made island. It would first be used for the fair and then become a world-class airport.

Building the island and fair was a monumental task, estimated to cost $50 million, but a welcome infusion of federal funding for the planned airport made it possible. Leland W. Cutler, a local businessman with extensive political connections, was hired to lead the effort, and work began to design and build the fair. It was quickly seen that meeting the initial goal of 1937 was impossible, so it was announced the fair would open in 1938. As it eventually turned out, the fair would open in 1939, putting it into direct competition with New York's fair. Luckily, having two fairs at the same time was not as much of a problem as expected; since the two events were on opposite coasts, visitors generally went to whichever was closer.

There were many differences between the two fairs besides location. The New York event was much larger, and major corporations spent lavishly on huge pavilions with widely varying designs. San Francisco went in a different direction, focusing much more on a unified architectural theme of coordinated buildings and gardens. Of the two fairs, the Golden Gate International Exposition was, by far, the more carefully designed and executed.

A few words on the naming of the fair: The formal title for the event was the Golden Gate International Exposition: Pageant of the Pacific. Over time, it had "1939" and later "1940" tacked on to denote the different seasons. It has also been called the San Francisco World's Fair, or the GGIE. I have used these names interchangeably, generally deferring to "fair," as that usage is the most common for such events in America, with "expo" prevailing overseas.

Speaking of names, credit is due to Clyde Milner Vandeburg for naming the site Treasure Island. Part of the fair's public relations team, Vandeburg came up with many of the names for the fair's courts, fountains, and streets. With Treasure Island, he evoked images of San Francisco's important role in the California Gold Rush, or perhaps Robert Louis Stevenson's novel and the 1934 film of the same name starring Wallace Beery and Jackie Cooper. The name was an immediate success and is still in use today, well after the fair.

The GGIE opened to great fanfare on February 18, 1939. There was daily coverage of the fair in the San Francisco newspapers, many of which printed stories urging people to come and enjoy the wonders of Treasure Island. Unfortunately, the crowds were less than expected, and despite the best efforts of the fair management to entice more visitors, they failed to come, resulting in a sea of red ink. Realizing that the fair would not make a profit, the organizers made the painful decision to cut it short by 34 days, closing on October 29. The story of the GGIE was not finished though, as explored in chapter three.

The fair's creditors may not agree, but by most accounts, it was a success. Press coverage was almost universally positive, and many printed accounts of visitor reactions showed they had a great time. A newspaper story in January 1941 noted that the fair had attracted 2,530,643 tourists from outside California who spent an estimated $328,762,470 during the 382 days it was open. Added to the amount spent by Californians, the fair certainly attracted new business to the Bay Area as the original backers had hoped.

In telling this story of the exposition, I have relied heavily on amateur photographs taken by paying visitors and only turned to publicity images for a few shots that have yet to surface in my own collection. As a result, I have focused on the buildings, the gardens, and the artwork of Treasure Island and not on the corporate displays of the latest electric toaster or powdered food. In today's world of free digital images on your phone and instant viewing of the results, it may be forgotten that in 1939, it cost close to $5 for a single color photograph. The photographers also had to carry some fairly heavy gear along with the film, then take it for processing, wait while they hoped it turned out okay, and finally find space to mount the prints in an album (or, like my family often did, stash them in a shoebox). All of the images in this book told a story for those who took them. I hope you will enjoy them as well.

—Bill Cotter
www.worldsfairphotos.com
September 14, 2020

One

BUILDING THE FAIR

Before construction could start on the new fair's structures, the island itself needed to be built. When the work began on February 11, 1936, the site was little more than rocky shoals ranging from 11 to 30 feet deep at low tide. A reported 260 tons of rock and 20 million cubic yards of sand were needed to create a 403-acre island 13 feet above sea level. Much of the rock used for the seawall was quarried from nearby Yerba Buena Island during the creation of a three-million-gallon reservoir designed to service the fair. The reservoir was filled with water that was carried under the Bay Bridge from San Francisco. All of that required more than 26 miles of pipes to quench the thirst of fairgoers.

As impressive as the building of the island was, and to complement the fanciful pavilions, the GGIE was designed to be visually pleasing, with a $1.3 million budget for the horticultural component. More than 4,000 trees, some between 35 and 75 feet tall, were moved to the site, along with 40,000 transported shrubs. An amazing 1.2 million flowers were grown especially for the fair to swath the grounds in a kaleidoscope of colors. At its busiest, this part of the fair alone employed more than 1,200 workers. The greenery required 50,000 cubic yards of topsoil to sit atop the compacted fill used to construct the island. For many visitors, the colorful gardens were the highlight of their day on Treasure Island.

During the early planning, the fair went by several names. Often called the San Francisco World's Fair, it was referred to as the World's Fair of the Pacific in federal documents authorizing funding in 1935, and later the World's Fair of the West. A contest held to formally name the event drew more than 12,000 entries. On June 3, 1936, it was announced that Elizabeth Whitney had submitted the winning entry—Golden Gate International Exposition: Pageant of the Pacific. Numerous others had suggested one half of the name, but she was the only entrant with the whole title. Her reward was a season pass and a part in the opening day ceremonies.

The Panama-Pacific International Exposition of 1915 had been a great success and helped to develop what is now known as the Marina district of San Francisco. The backers of the GGIE saw it as a sign that their new fair could also change the city's landscape. Some thought was given to using the 1915 site again, but by this time, the area was too well developed.

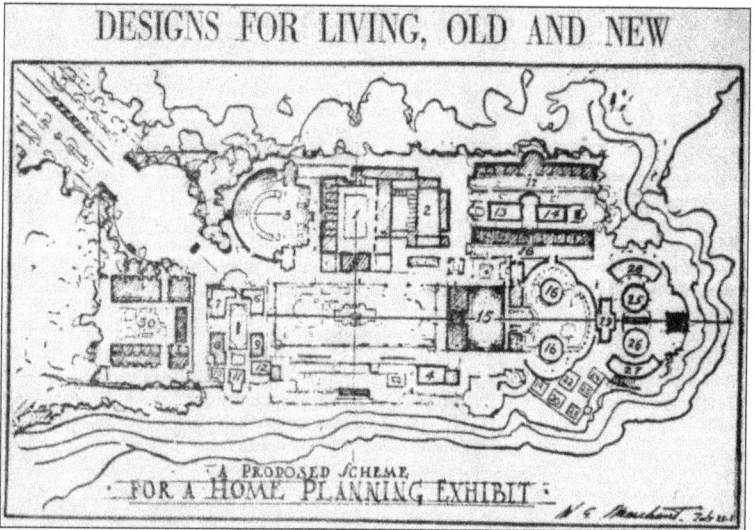

DESIGNS FOR LIVING, OLD AND NEW

A PROPOSED SCHEME FOR A HOME PLANNING EXHIBIT

The fair went through many design iterations before the final theme and physical plan were approved. Newspapers for July 28, 1934, carried lengthy stories on one major component that was eventually greatly reduced in size, a Furniture and Home Distribution Exposition. Architect William Gladstone Merchant described how his concept would showcase homes from around the world and throughout history. At this point, the fair was still planned for a 1937 opening.

Snags with federal funding almost caused delays in beginning the building of Treasure Island, but a last-minute wire transfer allowed dredging to begin on February 11, 1936. The seagoing hopper dredge *Mackenzie* began work at dawn that day, and the race against the clock was on! It took 11 dredges with 1,000 men working around the clock to finish the job on September 4, 1937—one day ahead of schedule.

The creation of Treasure Island was carried out under the supervision of US Army engineers and was a truly massive undertaking completed in an astonishingly short period of time. The 403-acre site, seen here at around the halfway mark on August 20, 1936, was billed as the largest man-made island in the world. All of this land dredged from the sea had to be specially treated to remove the salt and other minerals so plants could flourish during the fair.

With a substantial portion of the island completed, ground-breaking ceremonies were held on August 22, 1936, a scant six months after work had begun. Here, Gov. Frank F. Merriam proudly turns over the first shovel of dirt using a golden spade. The festivities that day also included laying the cornerstone of the fair's administration building. With that, work began in earnest on the exhibit halls for the fair as well as the permanent buildings for the future airport.

After extensive work to build the site and compress the soil, construction began on erecting the structures for the future fair. The first buildings were those intended for permanent use after the event because they required more extensive foundations on top of concrete pilings. This December 1936 image shows some of the intricate framework for one of the planned hangars, each of which were 335 feet long, 287 feet wide, and 80 feet high.

During construction, the fair commissioned Chesley Bonestell of Berkley to do a series of paintings that transformed the architectural plans into more eye-pleasing renditions used to attract investors and exhibitors. This 1937 painting showcases the Tower of the Sun, the fair's theme structure. Bonestell became one of the world's top science fiction illustrators, acclaimed by many as the "Father of Modern Space Art."

Work on the fair buildings continued at a breathtaking pace even while the north side of the project was still being transformed from a watery waste into an island. This series of views is from June 6, 1938, just six months before opening day. Seen here is one of the hangars intended for use by the Pan Am Clippers, with the future passenger terminal in the background.

Although the pavilions that were constructed specifically for the fair were temporary buildings, they still had to be substantial enough to last safely through the event and to stand up to the wear and tear of millions of visitors. Most were actually rather simple wood-frame structures, but a healthy coat of stucco and a good paint job made them look both lasting and impressive. More than 10,000 wooden pilings, 90 feet in length, were used during construction.

While work continued on the buildings, the grounds were opened to organized tour groups that were treated to a sneak peek and a catered luncheon. This was a wonderful idea for the fair; not only did it help with the cash flow, but the visitors became unpaid goodwill ambassadors as local newspapers carried stories of their visits and sparked public awareness of the approaching fair.

The fair's most famous visitor during construction was Pres. Franklin D. Roosevelt, who made a brief 10-minute tour of the site while on a whirlwind trip to San Francisco on July 14, 1938. Pre-opening activities really ramped up on December 11, the first of three preview days, when more than 31,000 guests strolled the grounds. The buildings were still under construction those days and were off limits.

A major milestone was reached on December 15, 1938, when all of the lights for the Golden Gate International Exposition were turned on for the first time. This photograph of that night, taken from Yerba Buena Island, shows the Tower of the Sun and the Main Court on the left. The view across the previously dark bay must have been breathtaking, with more than 600,000 candlepower of light illuminating the new island.

Working at a feverish pace to open on time, it was inevitable that there would be accidents, but the overall safety record was quite good until the very end of construction. On February 17, 1939, the day before opening, several workers were seriously injured when this elevator on a ski jump failed. Worse, carpenter Charles Paldi suffered a fatal two-story fall while trying to complete one of the exhibits the next day.

At last, the former muddy shoals in the harbor had been transformed into the magical world of Treasure Island. The Tower of the Sun and other exotic-looking buildings beckoned temptingly to motorists on the Bay Bridge. Many eager fairgoers snapped views like this on the way to the fair. In just a few minutes, they would be in a completely different world.

The Golden Gate International Exposition opened to the public on February 18, 1939. Eager crowds poured through the gates starting at 8:00 a.m. and began wending their way across the site. VIPs gathered in front of the airport terminal building to watch as Gov. Culbert Olson turned a jeweled key at 10:30 a.m. to symbolically welcome the world to Treasure Island. President Roosevelt also addressed the crowd by radio.

The US Postal Service issued a bright purple commemorative stamp to honor the fair. It went on sale the day the fair opened, and eager buyers were able to get a special cancellation at the fairgrounds. The stamp was a hit with collectors and regular postal patrons; 114,439,600 were eventually sold. (It is Scott's Catalog No. 852 for any stamp collectors.)

There were 12,000 parking spots on Treasure Island, and fair designers did their best to make coming by car as easy as possible, but the only automobile access was by the Bay Bridge, which emptied drivers onto a narrow and twisting road that slowed traffic. Officials had learned a valuable lesson during the preview days when there were delays in reaching the parking lot once on the island, so traffic lanes were quickly rerouted to eliminate most of the bottlenecks.

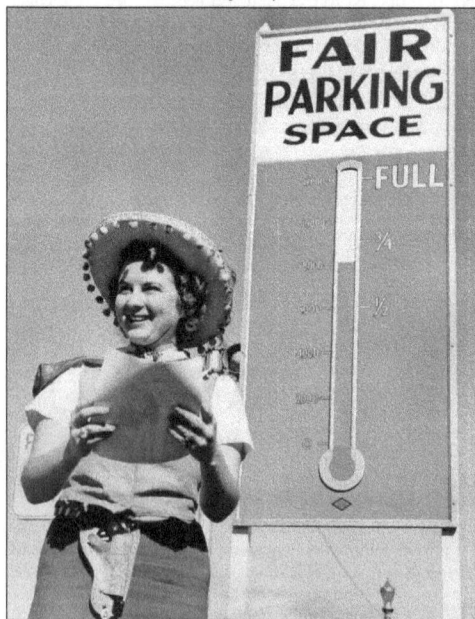

Pre-opening news stories about possible parking woes raised concerns that drivers might drive all the way to the fair only to find the lots full, so seven large signs were erected on roads leading to the bridge advising how many spots were left. The signs may have looked like they used the latest technology, but the "mercury" in the thermometer was actually a canvas panel moved manually by fair staffers. Model May Lewis is seen showing off one of the new signs.

Realizing that fears of traffic congestion on the bridge might dissuade fairgoers, special ferries were put into service from both San Francisco and Oakland. The adult fare was 10¢. The ferries were quite popular; daily attendance charts published in local papers showed that around two thirds of the crowd was coming by ferry for the 1939 season. Despite some long lines when folks headed home at night, it was still far easier—and cheaper—for most than coming by car.

A wide variety of other boats besides the scheduled ferries carried guests over to Treasure Island. The Port of Trade Winds Lagoon was often dotted with expensive yachts, and other visitors using docks such as this one arrived on smaller boats from all around the Bay Area. Fair records indicate that 517 people came by private boat on opening day alone, with a steady stream arriving that way throughout the fair.

Shortly after the fair opened, rumors began sweeping the city that inmates on Alcatraz Island (seen here from a ferry on its way to the fair) were trying to bribe guards for cells with a view toward Treasure Island. Warden James A. Johnson dispelled the stories in an interview on February 22, strongly avowing that the only time inmates could see the fair was when they were exercising in the prison yard.

The GGIE proved to be a hit from the start. It only took until March 15 to hit the one million guest mark when Betty Barnes walked through the turnstile. The lucky, but surprised, 25-year-old YMCA worker found herself honored with several parties and celebratory events and, best of all, showered with more than $1,000 in gifts.

Two

TOURING THE FAIR

After years of watching the expo being built, eager crowds descended on Treasure Island ready to explore the oddly shaped structures they had seen from the city or the Bay Bridge. The location meant they had to come by car, bus, private boat, or by ferry; no pedestrian access was available. For those coming by car, parking was 50¢ for up to five people and 5¢ for each additional person in the vehicle. The ferry to the fair cost 10¢ and an additional nickel for the ride home; there were many accounts of visitors who forgot to save something for the ride home, and that extra fare was eliminated in 1940.

Once on the island, admission to the fair was 50¢ for adults and 25¢ for children 5–12 years old. Guests could pick up an Official Guide Book for 25¢, or rely on a free map handed out at the gates. With all of that done, it was finally time to see the sights.

The expo grounds were laid out in a basic grid pattern, which lent itself to the rectangular nature of the man-made island, but finding one's way around was a bit complicated, as there were irregularly shaped buildings that blocked the way and a series of lakes to walk around. To make it easier to navigate, the site was broken into six central courts, and pavilions were broken into themed groups. Brightly colored signposts and helpful staff also made it easier, especially when using the soaring Tower of the Sun as a reference point.

At 403 acres, the GGIE was simply too much to see in a day, which was exactly as the organizers had intended. They offered numerous incentives to come back for another visit, such as heavily discounted tickets available through department stores and affinity groups, special children's days for only 10¢, and, best of all, free admission for servicemen in uniform during some events. Despite all of this, attendance was only about half of what had been predicted, meaning that on most days the grounds were relatively easy to navigate, and waits for shows and meals were quite manageable.

A cartograph of TREASURE ISLAND in San Francisco Bay
GOLDEN GATE INTERNATIONAL EXPOSITION

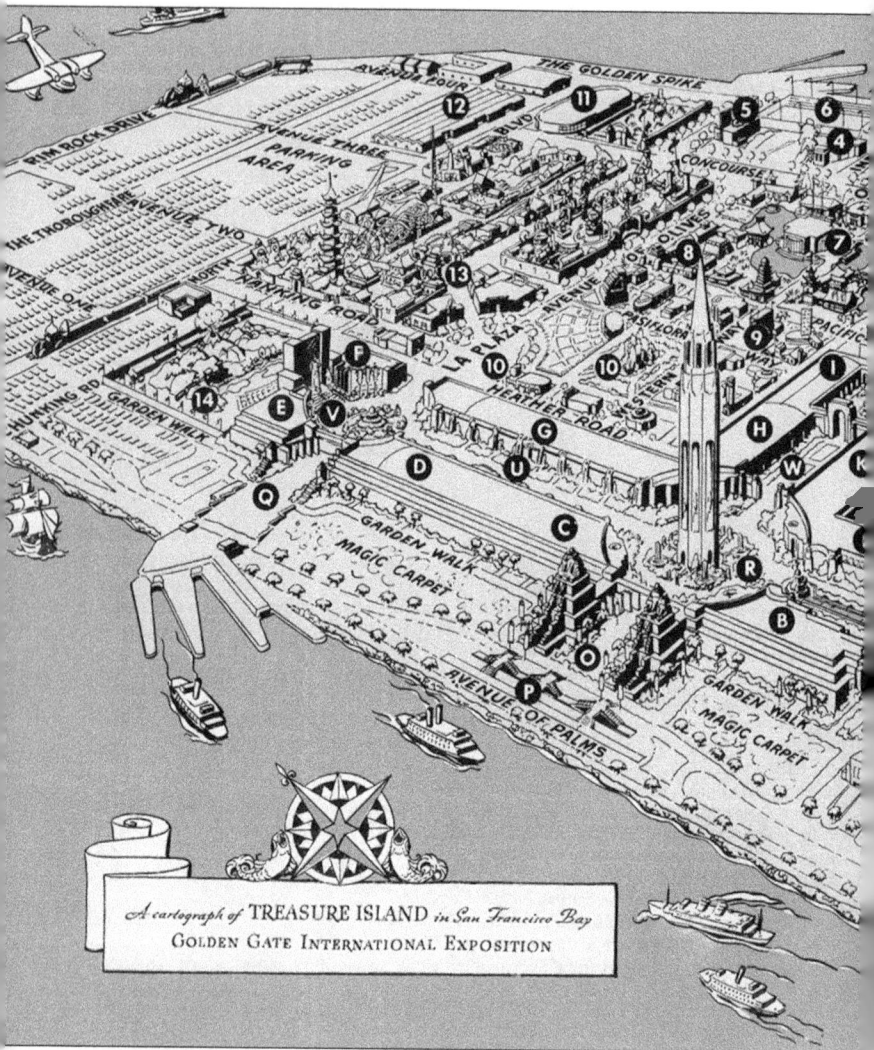

As this map shows, a trip to the Golden Gate International Exposition was quite an undertaking. This map may have been a bit fanciful—there were likely very few spouting whales and certainly no frolicking sea monsters—but it shows some of the wonders awaiting visitors when they arrived at this sparkling new addition to San Francisco. Some attendance numbers of note for the 1939

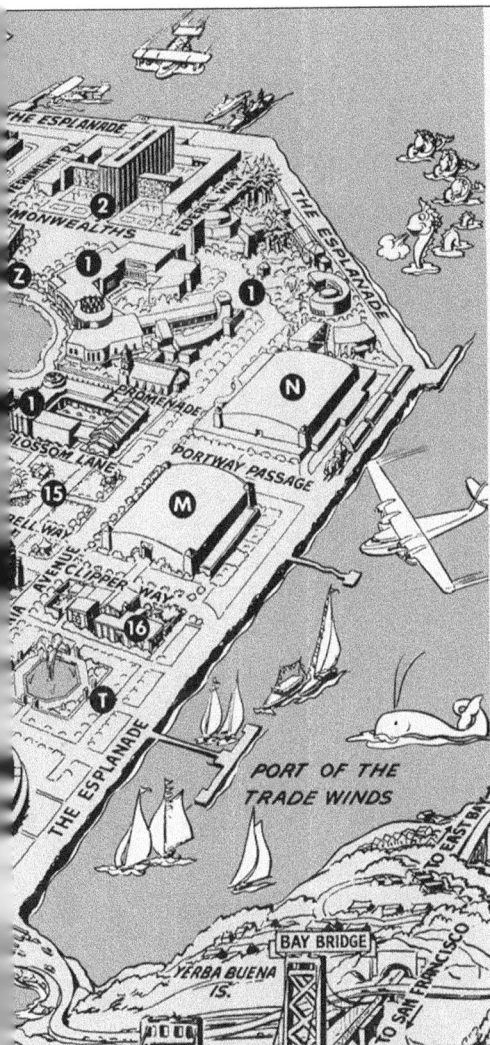

HOW TO FIND

BUILDINGS · COURTS TOWERS AND ZONES

Keep this map as a handy guide through Treasure Island. Find your locations by referring to the following key:

A   Administration Building.
B   Mines, Metals and Machinery Building.
C   Electricity and Communications Building.
D   Hall of Science.
F   Ford Building.
G   Vacationland.
H   Foods and Beverages.
I   Festival Hall.
J   Agriculture Hall.
K   International Hall.
L   Homes and Gardens.
M   Hall of Air Transportation.
N   Palace of Fine and Decorative Arts.
O   Portals of the Pacific.
P   The Sunset Bridge.
Q   Northwest Passage.
R   Tower of the Sun and Court of Honor.
S   Court of the Moon.
T   Treasure Garden.
U   Court of Seven Seas.
V   Court of Pacifica.
W   Court of Reflections.
X   Court of Flowers.
Y   Temple Compound.
Z   Court of the Nation.
     Lakes of the Nations.
1   California's Group of Buildings.
2   The Federal Building.
3   Hall of Western States.
4   Missouri Building.
5   Illinois Building.
6   Recreation Building and the Stadium.
7   Pavilions of the Pacific Basin Area.
8   Latin America Court.
9   Foreign Pavilions.
10   Central Square and La Plaza Groups.
11   California Coliseum.
12   Livestock Pavilion.
13   The Gayway.
14   Cavalcade of the Golden West.
15   Homeland.
16   Yerba Buena Club.

season were as follows: opening day (February 18), 128,697; slowest day (March 8), 10,259; busiest day (October 8), 187,730; and closing day (October 29), 147,674. The total for the season was 10,496,203, about half of initial projections.

The Golden Gate International Exposition may not have been the largest world's fair ever—the New York fair was three times the size—but it was still a considerable effort to see it all. The close proximity to San Francisco proper and the convenient ferry service made it easier to come back for the multiple visits it would take to fully enjoy all of the pavilions and shows. (Courtesy of Laurent Antoine LeMog.)

With the majority of visitors coming by ferry, this image shows how many of them would have started their day on Treasure Island with a view of the Portals of the Pacific, the western entrance to the GGIE. What mysteries awaited behind those forbidding fortress-like walls fronted by a line of palm trees? In just a few more minutes, the ferry would dock and the adventure would begin.

On their way from the ferry dock to the Portals of the Pacific, visitors were treated to the spectacular Magic Carpet, a 25-acre field of vividly colored Mesembryanthemum crystallinum plants. Commonly known as "ice plants," they do well in salty soil, making them a natural choice for the new man-made island. The area was awash in red, white, and purple flowers accentuated by the green plants underneath.

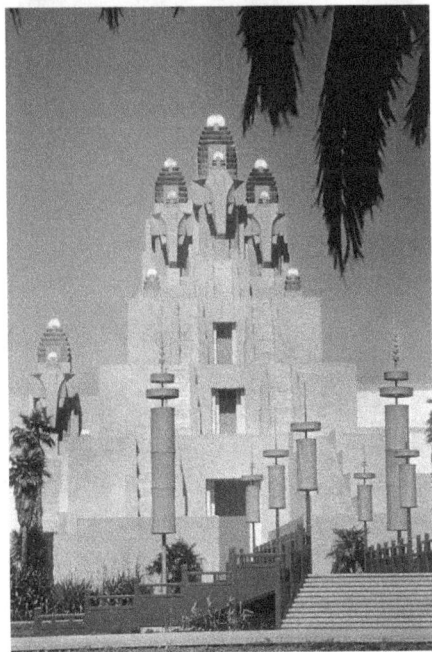

The Portals of the Pacific section was designed by Ernest E. Weihe, but the area is best remembered for the exotic Elephant Towers that flanked the entrance on either side. They were designed by Donald Macky and were a significant achievement for the young 26-year-old architect, a recent graduate of the California School of Fine Arts.

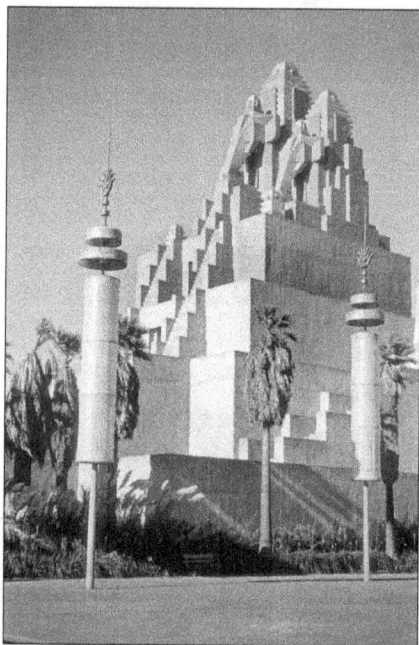

The towers stood 120 feet tall. The stylized elephants, with howdahs on their backs, were regarded as age-old symbols of pageantry. The towers themselves, with soaring faux staircases, were an intriguing mixture of Oriental design and Mayan architecture. Brightly colored, they were a tempting invitation to come in and see more of the fair. In retrospect, the elephants were a very unusual design choice, not generally being associated with the fair's Pacific motif.

Once on the island, visitors could tour the fair aboard one of the fanciful Elephant Trains. The articulated cab and trailers were said to resemble a line of elephants entering a circus tent. Powered by Ford V-8 engines, the unusually shaped tugs were actually built on a truck chassis. Guests could take a ride from the parking lot to the center of the fair for 10¢, and a scenic tour of the whole site was an additional 35¢.

It may seem quaint or even silly in today's high-tech world, but in 1939, the Elephant Trains were quite a hit. Visitors could ride a car or bus in most cities or travel by train, boat, or plane, but only at the GGIE could one ride in comfort in a gaily colored tram pulled by a mechanical elephant. The trains took in over $600,000 in 1939; that is a lot of rides.

Well-heeled guests could also travel the fair in style by renting an aptly named "roller chair." Pushed by guides who charged by the hour, the chairs offered tours that were custom designed to meet the schedules and plans of visitors. Many riders, though, balked when they learned that the guides had to be paid to wait for them while they toured inside the pavilions.

Another less popular conveyance was the rickshaws available outside the Chinese Village. Perhaps Western audiences felt guilty about being pulled around the fair based on depictions of low-paid coolies in movies, but in general, the crowds avoided them. The concessionaire staged a series of races to drum up interest, but they never caught on as much as the roller chairs.

Many visitors used the fair's theme structure, the soaring Tower of the Sun, as a focal point for their visits, radiating out to explore the site and then returning to the tower to set out in another direction. At 400 feet high, it was by far the tallest structure on the island and easily seen from all points of the site. It was designed by Arthur Brown Jr., the chairman of the fair's Architectural Commission.

Most of the temporary buildings on Treasure Island were wood frame, but the Tower of the Sun needed a steel framework anchored to heavy metal pilings in order to be so tall and yet so thin. The impressive tower was only 57 feet wide at its base. Wood sheathing was used to give the tower substance, and an outer coating added additional texture.

The Tower of the Sun held a 44-bell carillon that had originally been ordered for Grace Cathedral in San Francisco. When the church was not finished on time, the bells were loaned to the GGIE and then later installed in their permanent home in the cathedral in 1940, when the fair closed. The system was played from a keyboard at the tower base.

While most of the courts at the fair were centered on flowing fountains, the water in the Court of Reflections consisted of two quiet reflecting pools. In the background, partially visible behind the Arch of Triumph, were the Court of Flowers, the Lakes of the Nations, and the Federal Building.

Seen standing serenely at the end of the Court of Reflections, the 105-foot-tall Arch of Triumph was the end product of a talented team. The architect was Lewis P. Hobart, who also designed Grace Cathedral. There were two murals by Hugo Ballin inside the 90-foot arch and two stylized eagles by Jacques Schnier on either side.

The twin east towers of the Temple Compound stood on either side of the other entrance to the Court of Flowers, with the Lakes of the Nations off to the right of this shot. The unusual towers, designed by William G. Merchant, very effectively disguised the fact that the Homes & Gardens and the Foods, Beverages, & Agriculture Buildings behind them were fairly uninteresting structures full of industrial exhibits.

While attendance was generally way below what the organizers had hoped for, some events drew large crowds, as seen in this view of the Temple Compound. Temporary seating was used for events held at the Lakes of the Nations, but it was not enough for everyone; guests were jammed on the stairs and every other available space. If there had been more days like this, the GGIE would certainly have turned a profit.

Radiating out to the north of the Tower of the Sun was the 1,000-foot-long Court of the Seven Seas, the fair's most impressive thoroughfare. On the left were the Electricity and Communications Building and the Hall of Science, on the right was Vacationlands, and at the end was the towering statue of *Pacifica*. The exhibit halls were topped with stylized galleons to give the area a nautical touch.

This aerial view shows how large the Court of the Seven Seas was. Most of the fair's industrial exhibits were held in either these buildings or the two branching off to the left. As with the Temple Compound, imaginative design elements and sculptural pieces on the facades created an environment in which guests never really focused on the buildings themselves.

Inside the halls, a myriad of companies eagerly showed how their products were making lives better. Here, a model of a modern refinery is seen as part of the Standard Oil display inside Vacationlands. While such a display may seem of little interest today, visitors were eager to learn more about the infrastructure needed to support everyday lives.

Pacifica was the work of Ralph Stackpole, who went through 50 different designs before settling on this impressive figure who watched serenely over her domain. The statue was 80 feet tall and stood before a glittering "prayer curtain" of wind chimes that measured 100 feet high by 48 feet wide. The statue was destroyed after the fair, but the same design was later used on the city seal for Pacifica, California.

At the feet of *Pacifica* were doors leading into a 7,000-seat amphitheater used for the stage show *The Cavalcade of the Golden West*, written by Art Linkletter. The 75-minute show featured major milestones in western history. In 1940, the show became *America! Cavalcade of a Nation* and included scenes of famous events such as Valley Forge and Gettysburg.

The buildings around the Court of Pacifica were emblazoned with the names of famous explorers and were designed to act as windbreaks for the strong breezes that would blow across the bay. They proved to be too effective, so the chimes behind *Pacifica* did not work until small motors were added to make the curtain vibrate. The Fountain of Western Waters was at the center of the court.

One of the buildings around the fountain was the Ford pavilion. The 42,000-square-foot exhibit demonstrated many of the scientific instruments used to design and build modern cars. Raw products from 11 western states were shown being transformed into car parts on rotating platforms. The latest Ford cars were also on display.

The Music Hall, left, had an interesting path to existence. It was not in the Official Guide Book, as the space had not been leased when the fair opened, and it sat empty for several months. When the crowds were less than expected, a decision was made in June 1939 to offer more free entertainment. The Music Hall was quickly built and became home to big-name performers.

This view is from *Pacifica* looking back down the Court of the Seven Seas toward the Tower of the Sun. In the center was the Fountain of Western Waters, which was surrounded by a group of fanciful statuary figures referred to as the Court of Pacifica. They are described more in chapter four.

The Treasure Garden section, located behind the expo's administration building, was designed by George W. Kelham, who was also responsible for the Court of the Seven Seas and the Court of the Moon. There was apparently some confusion about the name for this area; newspapers and books of the time also refer to it as the Enchanted Garden, South Garden, and Sunken Garden.

The beautiful floral displays surrounding the fountains at the heart of the Treasure Garden were designed by Isabella Worn, the noted horticulture architect who had previously designed the gardens at Hearst Castle. Many official ceremonies were held in this area because it was just behind the expo's administration building. The Mines, Metals, and Machinery Building is to the left.

The gardens found across the site were one of the highlights of the GGIE. A great deal of planning and preparation had gone into their creation, and a veritable army of gardeners was employed to maintain them. GGIE management must be commended for keeping the gardens looking so attractive and not cutting back on this feature when they were forced to cut costs because attendance was less than predicted.

Recognizing that participating in the fair on their own might have been cost prohibitive for some counties, the State of California formed the California Commission and provided $5 million in funding. The commission helped groups of counties share buildings, often having to break political deadlocks along the way about what to exhibit, and then supervised the construction. A number of other exhibits, such as the California Building, were handled by the commission as well.

Nine Northern California counties banded together to sponsor the Redwood Empire exhibit, which touted the scenic attractions of the area as well as the value of redwood trees for building material. The entrance was styled after the famous Pioneer Cabin tree in Calaveras Big Trees State Park in Arnold, California, which had a tunnel carved through it in the 1880s to attract tourists to the remote area.

Zoe Dell Lantis, the GGIE's official "Theme Girl," poses climbing a redwood tree. A dancer with the San Francisco Ballet, Lantis traveled the country extensively in a variety of pirate-themed costumes to promote the event. She was so successful that newspapers dubbed her "the most photographed woman in the world." After the fair, she went on to a very successful career in aviation, both as a pilot and an executive.

Husband and wife team Irving and Gertrude Morrow were the architects for the Alameda-Contra Costa building. Their work included custom-made furniture throughout the building and the horticultural design for the surrounding gardens. Irving Morrow has a special spot in San Francisco history—he is credited with the orange paint scheme used on the Golden Gate Bridge.

With most of Los Angeles County paved over today in urban sprawl, it is hard to envision it as a major agricultural center, but at the time of the fair, there was a large agricultural presence that took full advantage of the sunny climate and imported water. The hall that included Los Angeles County also featured a collection by Cecil B. DeMille that showcased the area's important motion picture industry.

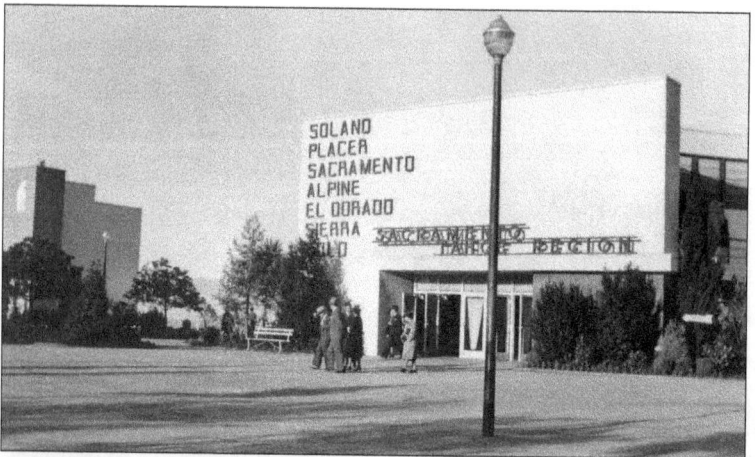

Six counties joined together to promote the agricultural and tourism industries of the Sacramento-Tahoe region. Live trout were kept stocked in a miniature lake, but the main attraction was $100,000 worth of gold. The display included gold in a wide variety of forms, including nuggets, dust, gold-rich quartz samples, and more. A special insurance policy was taken out for the exhibit.

The building also included a theater that showed travel films of the area that were specially shot for the fair. Color movies were still relatively rare outside of those shot in Hollywood, and the counties heavily promoted the fact that their films were in color. The theater was also used for performances and meetings by groups from the six counties.

Hoping to invoke thoughts of the majestic redwood forests in their counties, the Shasta-Cascade building featured a ring of trees around a campfire pit. It was a pleasant area to sit and relax away from the hustle and bustle of the fair. Inside the building, a series of dioramas with moving parts highlighted the commercial possibilities of the six California and three Oregon counties that shared the space.

One common theme shared by many of the California county exhibits was dioramas of their history and development. There were exhibits of indigenous settlements, explorer outposts and fortifications, early towns, farming, hydroelectric facilities, transportation systems, and more. All of these displays must have kept scores of model makers employed for years. Sadly, most of these miniature masterpieces were discarded at the end of the fair.

The California Auditorium, seen here at left, was designed to host radio shows and other live entertainment. Radio was king at the time, and the facility could handle 12 live broadcasts simultaneously. The largest studio seated 3,500. The facility also hosted a number of stage shows. The Federal Building is on the right.

Producer Clifford C. Fischer brought his show *Folies Bergère* from Broadway to the GGIE, staging it at the California Auditorium. Based on the shows at the famous Parisian nightclub of the same name, it enjoyed two very popular limited runs during the 1939 season. A new and expanded version returned for the whole of the 1940 season.

Folies Bergère was an elaborate presentation with quite a large cast. There were singers, dancers, burlesque comedians, puppets, and even trained dog acts, but the main focus was on elaborately costumed—or in some cases, barely costumed—showgirls. Critics were generally in favor of the show, and many commented on the difference between it and the nude shows in the Gayway area. (Courtesy of Vince Bravo)

The Mission Trails Building was a composite of the best features of seven of the Catholic missions that were instrumental in the settling of California. Some portions of the building used tiles and other materials imported from Spain, just as the real missions had, and there were numerous artifacts such as antique ox carts and religious items on display. Displays inside urged visits to the counties where the real missions could be found.

The host city of San Francisco celebrated its history with a variety of displays that showed major milestones such as the founding of the city, its important role in the famed Yukon gold rush, and how it developed into a major port for international commerce. The mayor of San Francisco had a suite of offices upstairs and entertained many of the dignitaries who came to town for the exposition.

The California Coliseum was another multipurpose facility built by the California Commission. The arena seated 9,476 and had a large oval track that measured 230 feet by 100 feet, with 12 lanes. It was used for a variety of sporting events that included track meets, bicycle races, and basketball games, as well as concerts and even rodeo events.

Early publicity material claimed that almost 40 states would be exhibiting at the GGIE, but in reality, only 14 participated in 1939 and 10 in 1940. Of those, most were smaller exhibits in the Hall of Western States. Missouri went in the other direction, spending $130,000 on an impressive 10,000-square-foot building that included a miniature Ozark mountain built of material trucked in from the real Ozarks.

The State of Illinois saluted its rich heritage with displays of early settlements and, as might be expected, a tribute to its most famous citizen, Abraham Lincoln. There were numerous maps and dioramas showcasing the state's industries and resources; the most impressive was a scale model of Chicago that included all 488,721 of the city's buildings.

The Hall of Western States contained exhibits from Colorado, Utah, Nevada, Washington, New Mexico, Arizona, Idaho, Montana, Wyoming, Oregon, and British Columbia in Canada, and California snuck in two displays on massive water projects underway in the state. The central courtyard displayed a giant relief map of the exhibiting states; a popular series of concerts was held there and in the building's auditorium.

The Temple of Religion and Tower of Peace was a privately sponsored nondenominational pavilion celebrating faiths from around the world. Historic artifacts were on display, and an outdoor garden featured 100 plants mentioned in the Bible. A 250-seat theater was the site of frequent choir performances, and Sunday worship services were held by leaders of many different faiths.

One of the island's two new hangars was used as the Hall of Air Transportation. The front portion held a variety of aviation displays, including the plane used by "Wrong Way Corrigan" on his infamous solo flight from New York to Ireland (he claimed he got lost on his way to Los Angeles). The rear portion was used by Pan American World Airways.

Treasure Island had been designed to become an airport after the fair closed, but there was actually scheduled air service during the GGIE. Visitors could tour one of the mighty Pan Am Clipper flying boats at the hangar or watch the craft depart on scheduled flights across the Pacific. The *California Clipper*, seen here, would be the last of the Pan Am Clippers to be retired when the service ended in 1946.

Pan Am offered two arriving and two departing flights each week for much of the fair, affording guests the opportunity to see the mighty Boeing B-314 flying boats in operation. Here, the *Honolulu Clipper* begins its takeoff run, racing to build up enough speed to spring free from the water. In just 16 to 20 hours, the passengers would be in Hawaii.

The Clippers required a great deal of maintenance between flights to make sure they were safe for their long over-ocean trips. After the passengers deplaned, the aircraft was hauled into the hangar for several days of work before the next flight. Special gantries and tooling were necessary to service the planes, which were some of the largest in the world. The hangars had been specially designed for just this purpose.

The Federal Building was truly impressive, measuring 675 feet long by 435 feet wide, with a commanding view across the Lakes of the Nations. Designed by Timothy F. Pflueger, the $1.5 million pavilion featured dozens of exhibits highlighting the work of many governmental agencies and programs. The complex received high marks from architectural and entertainment critics, many of whom proclaimed the money to have been well spent in educating the public.

The large open area in front of the building was originally named the Court of Nations but became better known as Federal Plaza. Many of the GGIE's major events were held here, including the opening and closing ceremonies, with scores of musical performances, military parades, and the political speeches that events such as the expo inevitably generate.

Twin murals designed by Herman Volz covered the front of each of the Federal Building halls. It took a large team of Works Progress Administration (WPA) workers to erect the murals, as each measured 360 feet long by 60 feet high. On the north building was *The Conquering of the West by Water*, with *The Conquering of the West by Land* on the south. These were the world's largest murals at the time.

The Colonnade of States stood between the two main halls of the Federal Building. The airy expanse was 265 feet long with 100-foot-high columns stretching toward the sky. There was one for each state, each decorated with that state's seal, and they were arranged in three rows to symbolize the executive, legislative, and judicial branches of the government.

Although the United States was not yet at war during the fair, there was increasing concern about its being drawn into the various conflicts already underway. Long lines formed behind the Federal Building to tour Boeing's experimental YB-17 bomber, which would evolve to become the famed B-17 Flying Fortress used to great success in the European theater. A total of 12,731 B-17s were built; this was the very first one.

The General Sherman tree is billed as the largest living single-stem tree in the world, so visitors were undoubtedly surprised to find a cross section of the trunk on display in the Sylvan Court section of the Federal Building. In reality, this was a replica, constructed to match scientific projections of the real tree's growth pattern. Markers indicated historical events that would have taken place at that point in the real tree's life.

Famous works of art, antique costumes, displays of textiles and tourism, and a theater showing films about France were some of the highlights of that country's impressive pavilion. The high point may have been Auguste Rodin's statue *The Shadow*, which was displayed in an impressive setting; additional French artworks were shown at the Palace of Fine and Decorative Arts.

Visitors looking for a fine-dining experience would often make their way next door to the Café Lafayette. The elegantly appointed restaurant hosted fashion shows during the day and a nightclub show in the evenings. A full filet mignon dinner might have set visitors back around $5. The restaurant made the news on August 5, 1939, when two "guests" left with $27,000 in jewelry that had been on display; the gems were recovered a year later.

The French Indo-China pavilion was lauded for the intricate wood carvings that were found throughout the richly appointed building. Artifacts from the ancient temple city of Angkor were shown, as were more modern pieces of lacquered furniture and other products from the region, which included rice, tin, coal, and rubber. That last very important import was on many minds as war clouds gathered in the region.

The soaring tower of the Netherlands East Indies pavilion drew visitors inside for examples of native craftwork, including batik dyeing, silver smithing, carved woodwork, and other skills. The gardens around the Japanese-Hindu–styled pavilion contained numerous examples of sculpture and stonework from the area. It was one of the highlights of the Pacific Basic section of the fair.

Fair visitors looking for something other than traditional American food may have found themselves next door at the 400-seat Javanese Restaurant. It became famous for a Dutch meal called *rijsttafe*, which was a 20-course rice dinner for two for $3. To make the meal even more memorable, each course was served by a different waiter.

San Francisco's large Italian-American community took great pride in Italy's pavilion. Huge letters, one foot thick, proclaimed the names of the country's major cities and regions on both sides of a 115-foot tower. Inside, travel films were shown, and hostesses from across Italy touted the wonders of their various regions. Artwork and photograph mosaics lined the halls of the building.

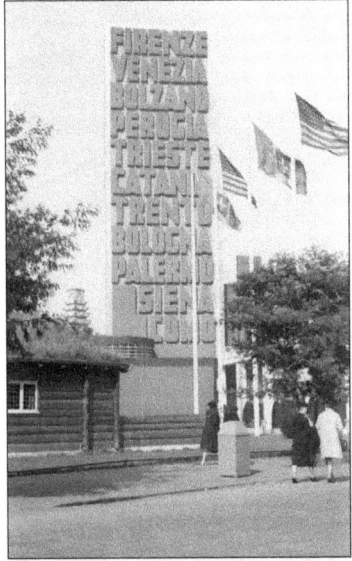

While most of the fair buildings were wood frame and covered in stucco, Italy made a show of economic strength by cladding its pavilion in marble quarried, of course, in Italy. Critics and historians took note of the effort and expense involved; one noted that "Quarries of marble revetment in the colonnade evoke Roman grandeur and civilization."

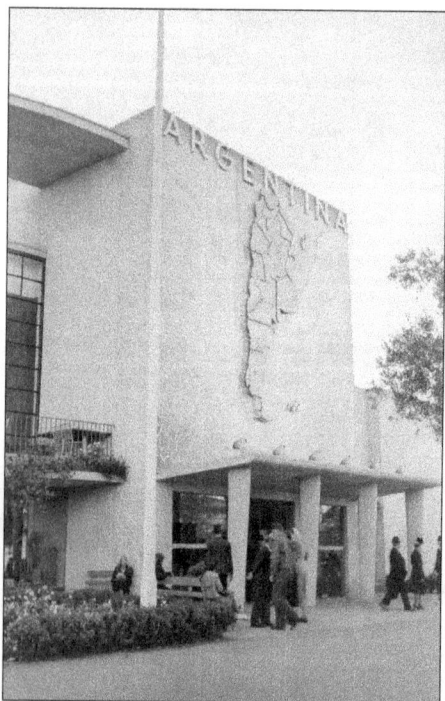

Noted Argentinian architect Armando d'Ans selected the International Modernism style for his country's pavilion. Built in just 59 days, the $200,000 pavilion featured a 160-seat theater, popular café, industrial and tourist displays, and, in a unique touch, a rooftop garden. A fine arts museum and well-stocked library highlighted the country's contributions to the arts.

Brazil had a very popular 25,000-square-foot pavilion that showcased the natural and economic offerings of the South American nation. One of the major attractions was a pleasant umbrella-covered patio where visitors could relax with a cup of fine Brazilian coffee as native birds sang from surrounding perches. Brazilian dignitaries and military leaders made several appearances during the fair.

Eight nations—Mexico, El Salvador, Panama, Guatemala, Peru, Colombia, Ecuador, and Chile—were located together as the Latin America Group. The area featured the attractive open-air Court of Hispania, seen here from the Lakes of the Nations. It was used frequently by performers from the nearby nations and immigrant communities now in the United States. The El Salvador pavilion is on the left.

The Mexico pavilion was quite popular, not just for the exhibits on Mexican history and culture, but most of all for a well-received restaurant that was said to have been one of the best food values at the fair. Mariachi and marimba bands also contributed to the ambiance. Mexican craftspeople were seen at work producing items for sale at the pavilion.

Coffee was the focus of the El Salvador pavilion. There were displays about how the beans were grown, harvested, and processed for brewing. There was also a café to enjoy hot or iced coffee, with the Sonora Marimba Band, musicians brought from El Salvador, providing live entertainment. Additional displays promoted the country's recent industrial advances.

Guatemala had a fairly typical pavilion with the expected displays about tourism and industry, but the most popular part of the facility was a simple wooden bandstand outside the entrance. There, the Guatemala Marimba Band entertained with performances every afternoon. The band had previously appeared at the Panama-Pacific International Exposition in 1915, and San Franciscans celebrated its return.

Panama had a large map showing how the world's shipping lanes converged on its famous canal. There were also displays of native costumes and early examples of jewelry and pottery. Outside, gardeners were kept busy trying to keep plants more suited to Panama's tropical climate healthy in the San Francisco weather.

Australia, seen here at far left, was part of the Pacific Group section. The pavilion had displays on the country's history, tourism, and products, but by far the most popular attraction was a small zoo featuring animals not generally seen in the United States at that time. Newspaper accounts told of visitors marveling at the kangaroos, wallabies, kookaburras, wombats, and exotic birds.

The State of Johore, part of today's Malaysia, had a spectacular display with a *dewan*, a recreated sultan's council house. Inside were displays on hunting, rubber plantations, and other industries, as well as some of the nation's crown jewels. A British protectorate, it was the first exhibit affected by the war, closing in early September 1939. In 1940, the building was operated as the Malay States pavilion.

One wing of the Philippines pavilion was devoted to the abundant natural resources and recreational offerings of the island nation. The second wing showcased products manufactured there as well as displays of traditional costumes and furnishings. An attractive bandstand in the lake behind the buildings featured concerts by the 110-piece Philippines Constabulary Band.

Japan went all out with its pavilion, second in size and cost only to the Unites States' Federal Building. The buildings were first built in Japan, then disassembled, shipped to San Francisco, and rebuilt there by workmen from Japan. The structures cost an estimated $500,000; additional sums were spent on the displays and operating expenses.

The Japanese buildings were described as a feudal castle combined with a Samurai house, surrounded by *kaiyu*-style gardens. When the fair ended, Japan offered the buildings free to any suitable taker, but as they had been brought into the country duty-free, they were burned down in May 1941 when no one could afford the customs fees. They were so strongly built that they survived a previous attempt to blow them up.

The rocks and plants surrounding the koi pond were brought in from Japan as well as the fish themselves. Thousands of Japanese lanterns were scattered across the grounds, adding an extra festive touch in the evenings. Unlike most of the other foreign pavilions, Japan did not tout its modern manufacturing facilities, perhaps to downplay them as the nation tooled up for war.

Inside, guests could tour a variety of exhibits proclaiming Japan's place as a modern nation. This sample living room featured Western-styled furniture rather than the traditional tatami mats, with hand embroidered art on the wall and colorful silk panels as accents. It is doubtful that most Japanese women of 1939 wore these costumes in everyday life.

Pacific House was a tribute to all the nations of the Pacific. The site had originally been slated for a very ambitious project called the Tower of Youth, which was to have served as the fair's theme structure. It was a joint venture between Bernard Maybeck, who had designed the Palace of Fine arts at the Panama-Pacific International Exposition, and William Merchant. When that project was abandoned, Merchant submitted this successful design for its replacement.

The building was beautifully set on the Lakes of the Nations. The Official Guide Book described it as the "theme dwelling" for the fair, but it failed to gain much traction in that regard, and the Tower of the Sun was seen by most to be the symbol of the GGIE. Pacific House is best remembered today for a series of murals by Miguel Covarrubias that depicted the Pacific Basin in colorful maps.

There were several ways to enjoy an outing on the Lakes of the Nations, including motorized boat tours with guides. The most popular craft were pedal-powered swan boats that were rented by the hour. Mayors of neighboring cities or competing organizations often challenged their counterparts to races in the fanciful craft, with their supporters cheering them on from the shore.

The Norwegian Ski Lodge was first built in Norway and reassembled at the fair by two craftsmen who traveled just for this project. Built from logs, the lodge was unusual in that no nails were used; the building was held together instead by its own weight. Visitors could enjoy Norwegian delicacies in a small snack bar or try out a sauna. The lodge is now a private residence in Salinas, California.

The 1933–1934 Chicago World's Fair had featured a number of very successful recreations of villages from around the world, leading one to expect a rush to create similar attractions for the GGIE, but there were only a few such exhibits. Here, a pitchman does his best to extort passersby to come inside the Chinese Village and see the wonders that await—for a small additional fee, of course.

Inside the formidable 45-foot wall, there were three acres of shops, shows, and restaurants. Of particular interest was a large exhibit of jade as well as silk clothing and other Chinese products. Performers from the village often paraded through the fair site to draw curious visitors back to the gates. The village cost an estimated $2 million.

The Territory of Hawaii had an impressive 21,000-square-foot pavilion that promoted the islands' tourism, sugarcane, and pineapple industries. Upon entering, guests were treated to a recreation of a steamship cruising past Waikiki and a 50-foot mural by noted painter Juliette May Fraser that showed the hookupu, a ceremonial presenting of gifts. There was also a 300-seat theater that ran a 10-minute color movie about the islands.

The Maori people and their culture were the focal point for the New Zealand pavilion. Styled after a traditional Maori meetinghouse, the building featured carvings and artifacts that stretched back to the arrival of the Maoris to the islands. Native dancers performed periodically, and guides were on hand to talk about life in the islands. Modern New Zealand was also represented by industrial displays.

Bank of America, which was founded in San Francisco as the Bank of Italy in 1904, was the only bank exhibiting at the fair. The bank spent $60,000 on its impressive building, a standalone structure that featured artwork on its windowless sides. A giant mural over the entry showed where the bank's branches were throughout California.

Billed as "The Bank of Tomorrow," the Bank of America branch was open until 10:00 p.m.—quite a rarity when most banks closed promptly at 3:00 p.m. each day. It was both a working branch, serving merchants across the exposition, and an exhibition of banking technology. A reported 3.75 million visitors toured it in 1939; more than 75,000 came in a single day.

The organization behind Sermons from Science has had pavilions at numerous world's fairs, beginning with the GGIE. Demonstrations explored the relationships between Christianity and science, with an exciting demonstration that sent a massive charge of one million volts of electricity through Irwin Moon, the lecturer. Surviving the blast, he then asked the awed audience, "Can you believe these miracles are the result of chance or accident? Or are they part of a divine pattern?"

The fair offered a wide variety of dining options, sometimes with multiple choices under one roof. The Continental Café offered two dining options. Visitors could get a full meal, including a cocktail, for under $1 in the coffee shop, or for about $2, one could enjoy a meal to the music of Les Smith and His 13 Boys in the full-service restaurant. (Courtesy of Vince Bravo.)

The Hall of Flowers was a very modern building and was quite a contrast to the rest of the fair. The 6,000-square-foot building featured windows of spun cellophane in wire frames that allowed sunlight to filter in and nurture the plants inside. There were flowers from across California and many others that were brought in from around the Pacific basin.

Gardening clubs and florists from across California were invited to exhibit at the Hall of Flowers, a wise marketing move that undoubtedly led many growers and their families to visit the fair. After the GGIE closed, the building was moved to the California State Fair in Sacramento; sadly, it was later demolished when that site was modernized.

A special detail of 32 members of the US Coast Guard were on hand to explain the service's history and important mission in protecting the nation's coasts and shipping industry. The building was located near the edge of Treasure Island, allowing for demonstrations of Coast Guard equipment and procedures just offshore. A "capsized" boat was recovered, and the "victims" received artificial respiration.

The waters around Treasure Island were often dotted with visiting Navy and Coast Guard ships, including several from foreign countries that stopped by on goodwill tours. With the newspapers full of stories about war in Europe and the Far East, there was increasing interest in these displays of military might.

Many companies and organizations celebrated special days at the fair, but it is doubtful anyone put on more of a display than the Matson Navigation Company. On August 9, 1939, the company sailed its liner *Mariposa* over at the end of a South Seas tour and moored it in the Port of Trade Winds. Every guest to the GGIE received a free lei upon entering the fairgrounds.

Unable to offer tours of the ship for logistical reasons, Matson more than made up for it with a series of lectures at the South Seas buildings about the ports it served, including a presentation at Hawaii by former governor Lawrence M. Judd. The high point for many was the free hours-long *Pageant of Matson Ports* stage show held at the outdoor stadium, which featured numerous acts brought in from the islands just for this appearance.

The GGIE brought San Francisco something never seen before in the city—and unlikely to be repeated! A tubular steel ski jump that reached 186 feet high was erected for the International Jumping Tournament. As the announcer claimed, it was likely the only time there was jumping on man-made snow on a man-made hill on a man-made island. Three hundred tons of ice were needed for the surface.

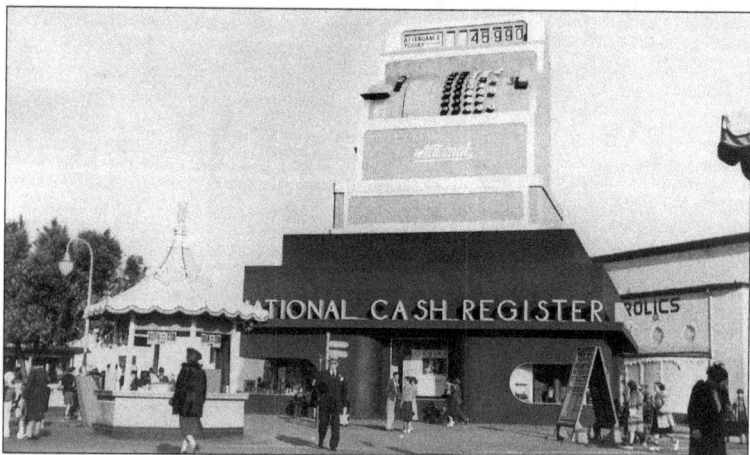

National Cash Register's giant register displayed the fair's daily attendance numbers and was updated every 30 minutes. It was as tall as a six-story building, and the numbers were more than two feet high. The lower levels showcased the company's business and accounting machines. National Cash Register previously had giant registers at the 1933–1934 Chicago fair and the 1936 Texas Centennial, with another one at the 1939–1940 New York World's Fair.

The bustling 40-acre Gayway amusement zone was touted as having something for everyone, from the risqué treats of the Sally Rand Nude Ranch at left to the more family-friendly Penny Arcade on the right. The latter is said to have inspired the 1941 Donald Duck cartoon *A Good Time for a Dime*. While the rest of the fair closed each night at 10:00 p.m., the Gayway stayed open until 2:00 a.m.

Jo-Jo the Clown was a very popular performer of the time; ceramic figures, paper dolls, and other merchandise bore his image. At the fair, he appeared in live shows billed as the *Candyland Revue* and also could be found between shows entertaining guests, as seen here outside the Construction Industries Building.

73

Those looking for some adventure and thrills were likely drawn to the Roll-O-Plane ride. It was built by the Eyerly Aircraft Company of Salem, Oregon. The company was originally formed to build flight simulators for the military but adapted its technology to a variety of aviation-themed amusement rides. Some Roll-O-Plane rides are still in use today.

Would-be aviators could also soar aloft on the Flying Scooter ride, which lifted them a few feet above the ground in a high-speed circle. For the more down-to-Earth types, there were plenty of other ways to have fun; the Gayway included a full-sized roller coaster, a miniature train, bumper cars, a fun house, the ever-popular whip ride, and more.

The twin Ferris wheels in the Gayway made the news on opening night of the expo when the power failed and stranded riders until a temporary electrical cable could be rushed into service. GGIE executives made sure the local papers all carried stories noting that steps had been taken to assure the problem would not happen again lest potential visitors be scared off.

Visitors interested in a plate of haggis or perhaps a fine Scottish malt could indulge themselves at a replica of a Scottish Clachan village. A variety of shops, even a post office, circled the traditional village green, which was well stocked with waterfowl. Craftspeople demonstrated various skills such as weaving cloth or Scottish dances.

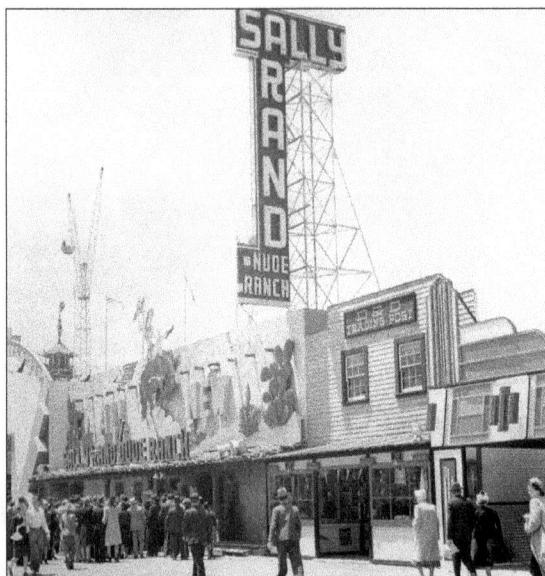

Sally Rand, who had made a small fortune with her nude shows at the earlier Chicago fair, came to San Francisco looking to repeat that success. GGIE management would only allow her to participate if the girls were kept out of public view, unlike at her show held simultaneously in New York, so they cavorted in various stages of undress in an indoor Nude Ranch. It was also a success. (Courtesy of San Francisco History Center, San Francisco Public Library.)

Incubators for human babies were relatively new, and amusement park operator Ed Breckenridge spent $75,000 to build an exhibit that invited fairgoers to "see a Cesarean operation performed before your very eyes" for 25¢. Once inside, they would discover this was on film and not a live operation. Eighty-five infants were cared for during the two years of the fair. The exhibit also included an iron lung, which was advertised as being available to anyone in the area in need.

Famous big game hunter Frank Buck operated one of the more popular Gayway exhibits, Jungleland. There were a reported 1.6 million paid admissions just in 1939. Once inside, guests saw a variety of animals Buck had brought from around the world on his many trips to supply zoos. Animal training demonstrations were given by members of Buck's team.

There were plenty of ways to get separated from one's money on the Gayway; bars and snack bars, thrill rides, nudie shows, games of chance, souvenir stands, and more. It looks like a lot of people were interested in getting their horoscopes as well. The whole area was loud, garish, boisterous, and fun. It was one of the most popular parts of the exposition.

Walt Disney produced his first animated commercial in many years for the Nabisco exhibits at the GGIE and the New York fair. Many books about Disney claim that *Mickey's Surprise Party* made its debut in New York, but the film actually opened at the GGIE on February 18, 1939, two months before New York. Disney is seen here (center) at the premiere with a Nabisco executive on the left.

Disney was also responsible for Mickey and Donald's Race to Treasure Island, a promotion held in conjunction with the Standard Oil Company of California. Children were encouraged to have their parents stop at a Standard station for the weekly giveaway, Travel Tykes, so they could collect the 36 coupons needed to fill out the border. The reverse featured the illustrated story "Mickey and Donald and the Nephews at the Fair."

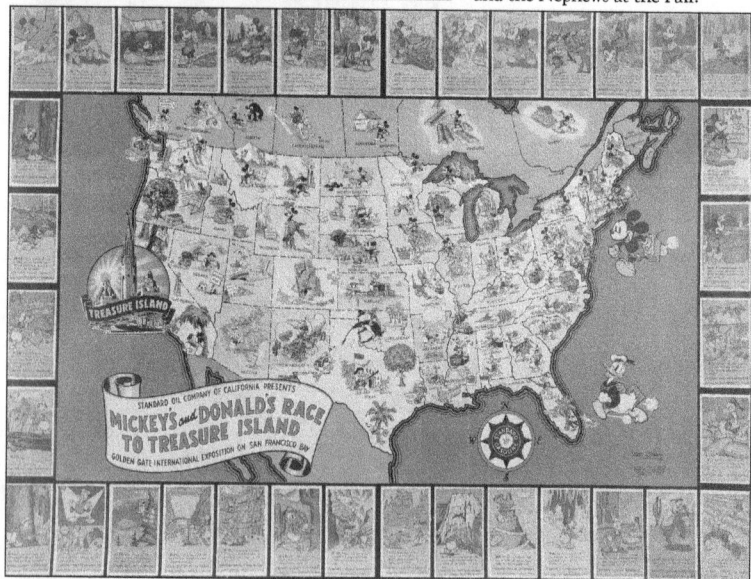

Three

THE FAIR IN 1940

When the exposition gates closed on the 1939 season, there was a great deal of confusion over what should happen next. The fair had lost $4,189,213.84, a considerable sum, but maybe there was a way to cut that figure down. The 1933 Chicago World's Fair had also lost money, but by cutting costs and reusing the already-paid-for infrastructure, its second season made a nice profit for its investors. Could the same magic work for Treasure Island?

One group of creditors, primarily the financial institutions that had bought bonds to finance the fair, was eager to cut its losses and be done with the whole matter. Other investors thought that there still might be a way to turn the expo into a moneymaker, or at least break even. A lengthy court battle ensued, one that is too complicated to cover in detail here. The end result was a compromise reached in December 1939. Those who wished to cash out their investment could do so for around 20¢ on the dollar, or they could roll the dice and see if the Chicago success could be repeated.

A new management committee was installed, and work began frantically on "The Fair in Forty." It was decided to offer a much shorter season, both to cut costs and because the late decision to reopen forced a delay in getting the site ready. Most exhibitors decided to return, and some, like General Motors, actually increased their presence. Sadly, a number of nations were unable to return due to the ongoing wars in Europe and Asia.

The fair management made many changes, such as reducing some admission and parking costs, adding new shows, repainting the island in a more vivid paint scheme, and launching a new advertising campaign to draw people back to Treasure Island. It was predicted that five million guests, about half of the 1939 numbers, would come through the gates. For once, the organizers underestimated, and more than six million attended. Unfortunately, this was not quite enough, and the second season also lost money. More court battles followed, and it was not until 1946 that the last bills were paid and the fair corporation officially dissolved.

How does an 80-foot-tall goddess get cleaned up after awakening from a long winter's slumber? For *Pacifica*, it required some help from the San Francisco Fire Department, which brought a ladder truck in for the job. High-pressure hoses were used to clean up *Pacifica* and the rest of the grounds. Happily, the winter weather had not caused undue wear to the temporary structures.

The new paint scheme on the exposition buildings was also reflected in the island's floral design, with many plants moved or replaced in order to complement surrounding structures. An army of gardeners worked right up to opening day to have the site ready for those anxious to enjoy another season of the GGIE. Here, the Court of Reflections gets a makeover.

Not everyone returned for the 1940 season. In most cases, their buildings were easy to repurpose for new tenants, but sometimes there was no disguising the fact that a building had been designed for someone else. In 1939, this dairy products stand had been the Dutch Windmill snack bar. After the fair, it was moved to San Miguel, California, for yet another lease on life; sadly, it burned down in 1978.

While the fair organizers did their best to group countries together based upon their real-world locations, sometimes countries ended up with some unusual neighbors. Here, Colombia and Switzerland share a common border; the latter had taken over a space formerly occupied by Chile and Paraguay in 1939.

Denmark took over the former Australia pavilion for some fairly typical displays of the country's products, but in an unusual twist, it also hosted a large number of musical performances by groups from across the Bay Area. Most were without direct Danish connections; the venue was available to a wide variety of performers. Piano and violin concerts were the most common.

Perhaps the most unusual reuse of a pavilion was the building originally occupied by France. When that nation could not participate in 1940 due to the war, the building became the home of the Treasure Island Ice Frolics. It was cost prohibitive to install ice-making machinery, so an artificial surface was used. The pavilion's show, *A Night at Lake Placid*, proved to be quite popular.

The former Yerba Buena Club was revived for the 1940 season as the Treasure Island's Women's Club. More than 11,000 members joined the club, which quickly became a popular dining destination for the city's business establishment, social elite, and visiting celebrities. More than 200 works of art lined the elegantly appointed halls and dining rooms, which had been redecorated for 1940.

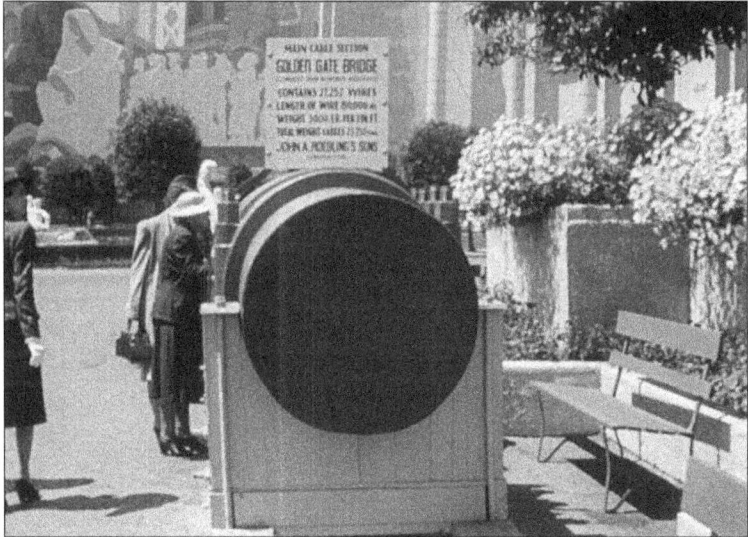

San Franciscans had watched the Golden Gate Bridge being built for several years, but most had not been able to see the work up close. A section of the main cable was put on display at the Court of Pacifica to explain how the mighty bridge had been built. This cable section is now at the visitor's center at the south end of the bridge.

Disaster hit the fair on August 24, 1940, when the California Building erupted into flames. The blaze was too large for the local fire crew, so 50 pieces of gear were raced across the bridge to join in the effort. The crew of two Navy destroyers anchored nearby and a contingent of soldiers stationed on the island also came to help, but the $350,000 building was declared a total loss.

Although the California Building was mostly destroyed, $150,000 of artwork inside was safely removed, and the adjacent San Francisco Building was saved. Important files from the offices were saved, but almost all of the displays were destroyed. The cause of the fire was never determined.

Republican presidential candidate Wendell Willkie made a stop at the fair on September 21 and gave a well-received speech saluting America's ability to carry out massive projects such as the GGIE. In an embarrassing moment, the official exposition band played "Happy Days Are Here Again" as he arrived, which had been President Roosevelt's theme song in the 1932 and 1936 elections.

A massive crowd turned out to see Willkie, and fair officials estimated that 30,000 of the 50,000 on-site at the time came to hear the speech. The burned-out remains of the California Building provided a somber backdrop for the event held in Federal Plaza. This may have been one of Willkie's more successful events; he lost resoundingly to Roosevelt, carrying only 10 states to FDR's 38.

The Federal Building focused heavily on leisure activities for the 1940 season, encouraging Americans to take up new hobbies and to travel across the country, two activities likely to stimulate the economy. A small lake was built to demonstrate the fine art of fly fishing; here, noted angler Joe Gomez prepares to demonstrate his ability to cast his lures at a distant target.

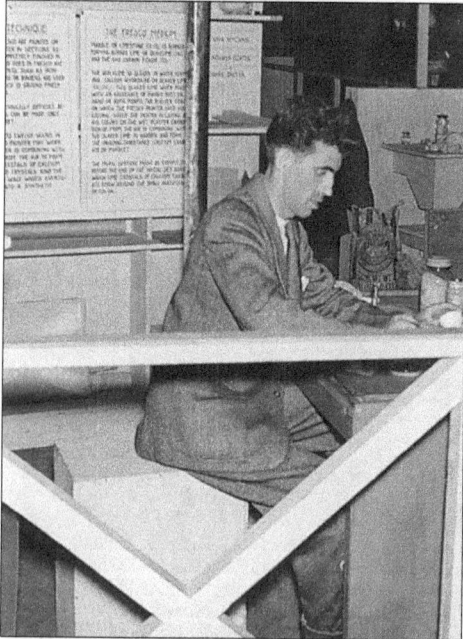

The foreign artwork in the Palace of Fine and Decorative Arts was returned at the end of the 1939 season, and the space was repurposed to showcase artists at work under the auspices of the WPA. Here, artist Diego Garcia is seen working on a massive mural entitled *Pan American Unity* to be installed at San Francisco Community College. For a number of reasons, the 74-foot-long mural was not installed until 1961.

In 1939, General Motors had a relatively low-key exhibit inside Vacationlands, and most press coverage about the auto industry exhibits at the GGIE focused on the much larger Ford display in its own building. This did not go unnoticed in Detroit, and in 1940, General Motors took over the former Music Hall to go bumper-to-bumper with Ford.

Flamboyant producer Billy Rose offered to run the GGIE for its second year but had to settle for bringing a new version of his hit water pageant *Aquacade* from the New York fair to San Francisco. A new 200-foot by 65-foot pool was constructed inside the former International Hall, and stars Johnny Weismuller and Esther Williams led a giant cast in a show that attracted close to two million spectators. (Courtesy of San Francisco History Center, San Francisco Public Library.)

As the threat of another world war continued to increase, the US military sponsored an increasing number of parades and demonstrations on Treasure Island. Displays of aerial acrobatics and visits by Navy ships also helped send the message that America was ready for war, and interested men could participate in recruiting drives. Unfortunately, the message failed to make an impression where it counted, and in a little over a year, America was at war.

Finally and sadly, after years of planning and building and millions of dollars in expense, the gates swung shut on the Golden Gate International Exposition for the last time on September 29, 1940. After picking up one last souvenir, the last of the 17,041,999 guests who had come to Treasure Island finally went home, and the Pageant of the Pacific was over.

Four

ART AT THE FAIR

From the very first moments the Golden Gate International Exposition was planned, it was known that art would be a major component of the event. The Palace of Fine Arts at the Panama-Pacific International Exposition had been one of the most popular venues at that 1915 fair, and decades later, art lovers were still discussing the magnificent collection it had housed. Now the city would have another opportunity to establish itself as a major art and cultural center through the new fair.

Several committees were formed to handle the formidable task of assembling a collection that could withstand the inevitable scrutiny of the art world and yet also be pleasing to the less discerning crowds who would be the paying customers of the GGIE. One of these groups handled the art that would be commissioned and paid for by the fair. A very impressive budget of $1 million was proudly announced, creating instant credibility for the fair. Some naysayers did harp on how many carpenters or other craftsmen could have benefited from having that money directed to more plebian projects such as housing, but for the art community, this was very welcome news indeed. Even with such a large budget, corners had to be cut, so most of the statues created for the fair were made out of plaster rather than much more expensive marble or granite. Several pieces that would be exposed to water from nearby fountains were cast in concrete; those are some of the few commissioned pieces that still exist today.

Other committees set off to borrow art from around the world for the massive Palace of Fine and Decorative Arts held in one of the two airplane hangars constructed on the island, or to search out works from California artists to showcase in that state's pavilion. When the work was done, and the art displayed, even the harshest of critics had to admit that the GGIE art teams had outdone themselves.

The *Fountain of Life* in the Court of Flowers stood 50 feet tall. At the top was the 12-foot statue *Girl and the Rainbow* by Olof C. Malmquist, which depicted a woman plucking a rainbow out of the sky. Many descriptions of the statue state she was nude, but in fact, she was clothed.

At the base was a group of smaller statues by Malmquist depicting mermaids and mermen frolicking with other sea creatures. Malmquist contributed several other works for the exposition, the most famous being the large *Phoenix* that stood atop the Tower of the Sun. It signified San Francisco's rebirth after the disastrous earthquake and fire of 1906, which had ravaged the city.

Malmquist was one of the most prolific sculptors at the fair. His 22-foot metal stylized *Phoenix* was made of wrought iron but gilded in gold to reflect the sun and look as if it were in flames. Malmquist also had several relief sculptures on the tower walls representing different types of wind. (Courtesy of San Francisco History Center, San Francisco Public Library.)

Closer to the ground and easier to see, the Tower of the Sun was adorned with a group of eight statues by sculptor William G. Huff. There were four figures, each 20 feet tall, representing industry, agriculture, science, and the arts. Two of each figure were needed to fill the arches in the octagon-shaped base of the tower.

Noted female artists Helen Forbes and Dorothy Puccinelli had worked together on a number of WPA projects, and joined forces again for a series of four murals titled *First Garden*. Located inside the south towers at the Homes & Gardens Building, the colorful works were based on Biblical themes with vivid plants and jungle creatures. One of Puccinelli's pieces is seen here. (Courtesy of Vince Bravo.)

St. Francis of Assisi, after whom the city of San Francisco was named, was the subject of this work by Clara Huntington. The bronze statue of the saint feeding birds looked magnificent surrounded by a sea of flowers in the Court of Honor. It is now located in the Fragrance Garden in Golden Gate Park.

Pantheon de la Guerre was a major art addition for the 1940 season. Taking up half of the former Mines, Metals, and Machinery Building, it was a massive diorama of major battle scenes from the first world war and had originally been seen at the 1933–1934 Chicago World's Fair.

The *Spirit of Adventure* figures were at the front of the galleon figures created by P.O. Tognelli on the Court of the Seven Seas. There were 16 of these soaring 60 feet high and lining the court. In 1937, Tognelli and seven assistants had built the official model of the GGIE that was used for design and publicity purposes. The massive model measured 29 feet by 18 feet.

While most of the statues on Treasure Island were white, as they were made of plaster or concrete, Tognelli's *Discovery* over the entrance to the Vactionlands hall in the Court of the Seven Seas was painted gold. It looked particularly impressive when lit at night. The piece featured a figure of an explorer emerging from the bas-relief background.

One of the entrance doors to the Temple Compound displayed the intricate carved details that made the GGIE so intriguing. This section of the fair was designed by William G. Merchant and was quite a contrast to his modern-looking Pacific House. Merchant also served on the Architectural Commission that oversaw the look of the entire exposition.

To many, the grounds themselves were a work of art. There were very few barren spots on Treasure Island. Instead, there was a profusion of plants and gardens, with fountains of all types to attract the eye. Some were majestic soaring jets of water such as in the Treasure Garden, and others, like this, a quiet spot to sit and relax.

When the expo closed, little thought was given to preserving the artwork that had delighted so many. As their counterparts in New York also found, the artists discovered that the plaster pieces had suffered a great deal of wear and tear after two years of being exposed to the elements. Perhaps more would have survived if there had only been one season. This was *The Earth Dormant* by Haig Patigian.

Rain was another Patigian sculpture and like *The Earth Dormant* was part of a group of four statues located at the four corners of the Treasure Garden. The other two pieces were called *Sunshine* and *Harvest*.

The widow of recently deceased sculptor Edgar Walter loaned his bronze work *The Girl and the Penguins* for exhibition in the Court of Reflections. It was a difficult piece to photograph down the length of the long reflecting pool, so most images only show her derriere through a mini forest of aquatic plants. Luckily, one photographer caught her good side.

Paul Manship's *Celestial Sphere* stood at the entrance to the Palace of Fine and Decorative Arts. It was a copy of an armillary sphere he had crafted for the Woodrow Wilson Foundation for display at the League of Nations in Geneva. Manship also had another copy on display at the New York fair, possibly making him the only artist represented at both events.

The outside may have looked like an aircraft hangar, but inside, the palace looked like a high-end art museum. A panel of experts had scoured the world and assembled a collection that was valued at either $20 million or $40 million depending on the source. Attendance started off slowly due to the additional admission fee, but as word spread, the palace became a must-see for many fairgoers.

This piece by Haig Patigian, a two-time president of the Bohemian Club who was born in Armenia, had actually been created for the Panama-Pacific International Exposition of 1915. It survived the destruction of that fair for it had been cast in bronze, unlike many of the temporary pieces of art on display there. It was donated to the Bohemian Club in 1921 by Amelia Pixley, widow of prominent member Frank Pixley, and later loaned to the GGIE.

Haig Patigian had a new piece at the GGIE, this 16-foot sculpture titled *Creation*. It featured a nubile young woman, a brawny man, and an old woman, all representing the circle of life. Patigian snuck himself into the piece as the kneeling sculptor creating the work. A five-foot artist's model of *Creation* made the news when it was stolen from a San Francisco yard in 1955 as a prank by football players; happily, it was recovered undamaged.

Lady of the Lamp, a tribute to Florence Nightingale, was created in 1937 by David Edstrom as part of a WPA project. Sadly, he died in 1938 and did not see his work at the GGIE. The statue of the founder of modern nursing was unveiled in the Court of the Seven Seas in front of 1,100 nurses on May 12, 1939, Nightingale's 119th birthday. It is now on display at Laguna Honda Hospital in San Francisco.

Another statue was added to the fair after opening day. This one honored the National Guard of California and was dedicated on May 31, 1939. The inscription on the base read, "For Country and Humanity." After the GGIE closed, it was transferred to Capitol Park in Sacramento.

Representing the winds of the Pacific, *Ocean Breeze* by Jacques Schnier was just one of a number of statues that raised concerns for the GGIE's general manager, Henry Connick. Connick told reporters that he was worried that the authorities might raid the fair and shut it down due to the nudity depicted. He proposed covering the women, but the artists prevailed, and the pieces were displayed as intended.

The Fountain of the Evening Star was topped by Ettore Cadorin's *Evening Star* at the southern end of the Court of Honor, facing the reflecting pool in the Court of the Moon. This was another of the statues that caused Connick grief; as it turns out, he was let go during the 1939 season for being too conservative in his choice of entertainment used to attract crowds.

Ettore Cadorin had another piece at the opposite end of the Court of the Moon. *The Moon and the Dawn* was a whimsical piece showing two figures looking wistfully at each other as night gives way to a new day. Although the full-sized statue seen here did not survive the demolition of the fair, the artist's original model of the work was saved and still exists today.

Many of the exhibit buildings were works of art in their own right. The Homes & Gardens Building, seen here, was part of the Court of the Moon. This section was one of the areas designed by George W. Kelham, chief architect of the exposition until his death in October 1936. Kelham imbued his creations with a mix of Mayan, Incan, Malayan, and Cambodian architecture with a few modern touches.

Pioneer Mother by Charles Grafley had a very unusual path to the fair. The bronze sculpture had been created for and exhibited at the Panama-Pacific International Exposition in 1915, then was somehow left behind in the ruins of a building from that fair for more than 20 years. When finally found, it was refurbished and displayed prominently at the GGIE. It is now in Golden Gate Park, the only statue of a woman there.

The Pacifica Group of statues was the largest collection of sculptures with a unified theme at the fair. A total of eight artists contributed 20 figures that ringed the Fountain of Western Waters at the base of Ralph Stackpoole's towering Pacifica.

Several sculptors were engaged to create pieces for the Fountain of Western Waters in the Court of Pacifica. *Young Native Riding an Alligator* by Cecilia Bancroft Graham was part of the South American Group. This is one of the few surviving pieces of sculpture created for the fair. In the background is one of the North American Group figures, *Mexican Boy Resting on His Burden* by Ruth Cravath Wakefield.

Carl George's *Modern American Woman* was one of the most impressive pieces in the Pacifica Group collection. While many of the others works had a whimsical tone to them, this one portrayed a feeling of strength, progress, and determination. George also created a statue of a Native American woman in the same area.

Brents Carlton sculpted this piece titled *Polynesian Girl* of a young woman holding a stalk of bananas or plantains. There was also a companion piece, *Polynesian Boy*. Carlton was primarily a painter but had switched to sculpture at the time of the GGIE, later returning full time to painting.

Sargent Johnson contributed two pieces to the same fountain of Incan boys riding llamas. The eight-foot-high sculptures evoked criticism from some who claimed llamas cannot be ridden. It turns out Johnson did his homework, for the animals can support the weight of children but not adults. The boy and his llama seen here both seem happy with the arrangement.

Three sisters—Esther, Margaret, and Helen Bruton—were awarded a contract for $20,000 for the massive mural *The Peacemakers*, which dominated the western side of the Court of Pacifica. At 144 feet long and 57 feet high, it was constructed in 270 panels made of layers of Masonite carved to produce the striking three-dimensional look seen here. It took the sisters nine months to create the mural, the largest at the fair.

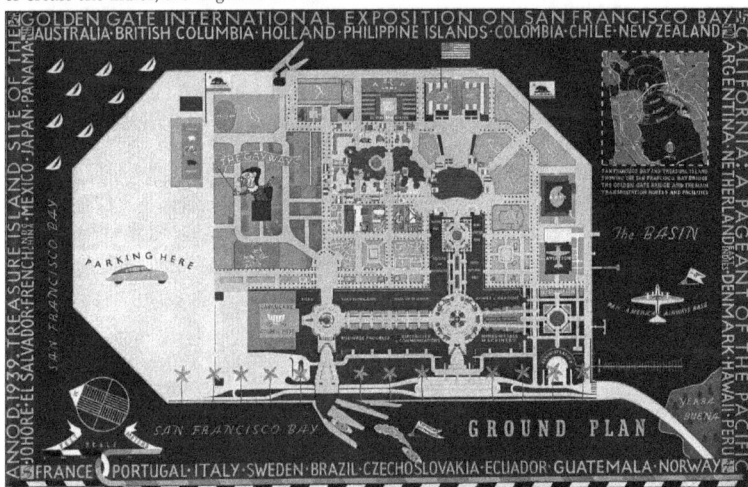

Architect Ernest Born, who served as an architect on the California Building and selected works for the Architecture Division in the Palace of Fine and Decorative Arts, was also an accomplished muralist. This exquisite map of the GGIE by Born was located in the Court of Pacifica and measured approximately 20 feet across. Painted in vivid colors, it helped fill an otherwise empty wall to great effect.

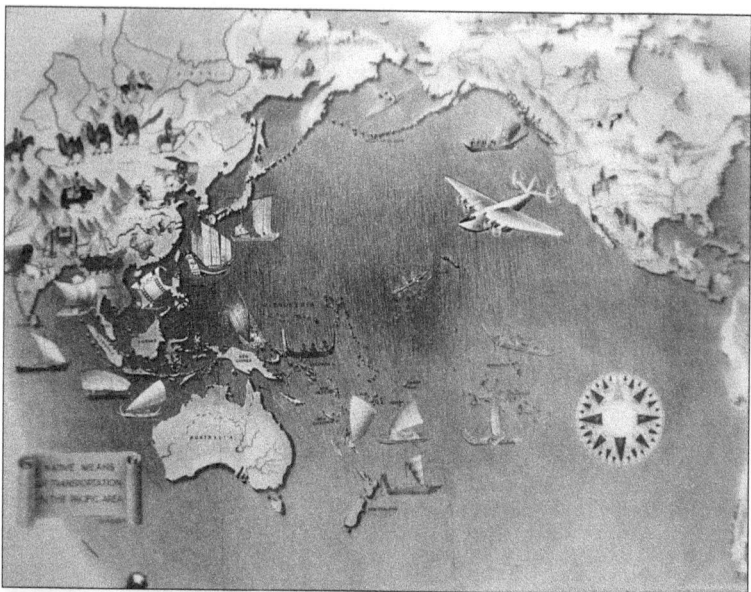

Miguel Covarrubias produced some of the most critically acclaimed pieces of art at the GGIE in a series of murals that adorned the walls inside Pacific House. In this one, *Native Means of Transportation in the Pacific Area*, natives are seen traveling between the islands in a variety of canoes, rafts, and small boats. Overhead, a mighty Pan Am Clipper is seen bringing a new way of travel to the once remote islands.

Brents Carleton also did a pair of carved 18-foot plaster figures that adorned the California building. A similar figure of a woman was on the other side of the structure. Carleton's original maquette of this figure of a man with a hook and chain and a sledgehammer is now in the Wolfsonian collection at Florida International University in Miami, Florida.

Noted muralist Hugo Ballin decorated the inside of the Arch of Triumph with two panels of a mural he called *The Winds*. Ballin explained his inspiration for the work saying, "Men would never have sought new lands had not the winds of heaven whispered to them." Each of the panels was 45 feet high and 10 feet wide. (Courtesy of Vince Bravo.)

In addition to all of the art commissioned by the GGIE and prominently displayed in the public spaces of the fairground, there was a considerable amount of art at the international and commercial pavilions. Intricate carvings such as this piece at New Zealand often used woods and other materials or techniques not generally employed in the United States, adding an interesting aspect to many works of art.

The Brazil pavilion featured two striking murals, one on either end; surprisingly, they were done by American artist Robert Howard, not by a Brazilian. Howard contributed several other murals and sculptures to other locations at the fair, and his wife, Adaline Kent, sculpted pieces for the Pacifica Group of figures. (Courtesy of Vince Bravo.)

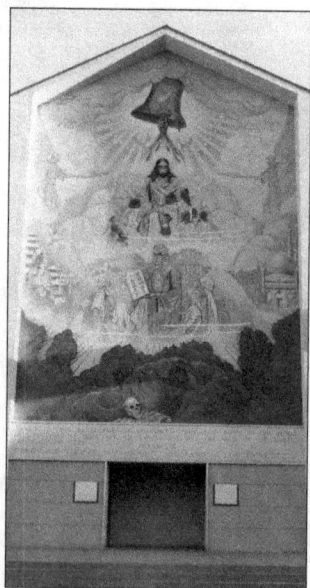

This work by Peter A. Ilyin, *The Evolution of Religious Freedom*, was over the entrance to the Friendship Hall at the Temple of Religion. Leading up from the doorway were two Biblical quotes and then vignettes showing the effects of war and slavery, the Giving of the Law, the Sermon on the Mount, and an overarching Liberty Bell motif. Ilyin also had two murals in the San Francisco Building and seven in the Dairyland Building.

Louis Siegriest created a series of eight posters for the Indian Court at the Federal Building. Based on a combination of ancient Native American motifs, the silk-screened posters were a huge hit with fair visitors, art lovers, and historians. The government gave away more than 1.25 million at the fair and afterwards. Requests were still coming in when the supply finally ran out. The posters are worth quite a bit on the auction market today.

ANTELOPE HUNT FROM A NAVAHO DRAWING · NEW MEXICO

INDIAN COURT
FEDERAL BUILDING
GOLDEN GATE INTERNATIONAL EXPOSITION
SAN FRANCISCO 1939

Starting JUNE 15th
FEDERAL THEATRE
TREASURE ISLAND
SWING MIKADO
A CAST OF 100
Sensational Success
HOT FROM NEW YORK
daily PERFORMANCE 8 P.M. (EXCEPT MON.)
PRICES 25¢ 50¢ 75¢ PLUS TAX

THE BIG HIT OF THE
GOLDEN GATE INTERNATIONAL EXPOSITION

A DIVISION OF THE
WORKS PROGRESS ADMINISTRATION

There were other art forms at the GGIE besides sculptures and paintings. A number of well-received shows were staged in the theater at the Federal Building under the auspices of the WPA through the end of July 1939, when the WPA theater program was dissolved. After that, the theater was used for a series of unremarkable government films.

109

When a large number of government agencies had to pull out of the Federal Building for the 1940 season because they had not budgeted for the year, the gap was filled by the WPA. The agency put an emphasis on art and recreation as part of the government's efforts to bolster the economy through increased family spending. Here, a group of tourists passes by a WPA poster just inside the turnstiles that advertises an upcoming concert at the fair.

THE GOLDEN GATE INTERNATIONAL EXPOSITION
and
TWENTIETH CENTURY-FOX FILM CORPORATION
present the
GALA PRESS PREVIEW
of Darryl F. Zanuck's Production of
"THE STORY OF ALEXANDER GRAHAM BELL"
A Cosmopolitan Picture

Treasure Island   Federal Theatre
March 29, 1939

Hollywood came to the GGIE—well, almost. The film *Charlie Chan at Treasure Island* (1939) was supposedly set at the GGIE, but the fair only appeared in a few brief moments of stock footage. Hoping to maximize interest in its new movie *The Story of Alexander Graham Bell* (1939), 20th Century-Fox held a lavish press preview at the GGIE before the official world premiere a month later at the New York fair.

Five

THE FAIR AT NIGHT

Lighting Treasure Island was a daunting task. The site had to be bright enough to walk through safely at night but not so bright as to distract from the fanciful buildings that were the heart of the fair. All of the lighting had to complement the color schemes of the buildings and gardens. Most people never give it any thought that artificial light is a completely different color spectrum than natural daylight. The size of some of the structures was also a formidable challenge, one the GGIE met head on.

The fair organizers allocated $1 million to the lighting project and engaged the services of A.F. Dickerson from General Electric, one of the company's leading experts in the field of architectural lighting. Dickerson worked closely with Jesse E. Stanton, the fair's color architect, to craft a color palette that was not only attractive, but could also be executed as subtly as possible.

In order to achieve this, careful consideration was given to the buildings themselves. Almost every building on the island was constructed without windows, providing a canvas for painting them with color without the distraction of interior lights jutting into the scene. The plaster was infused with vermiculite to subtly reflect the light back toward the viewer, which made the buildings seem to sparkle and glimmer. Fluorescent paint was sometimes used, providing an unusual look when bathed in ultraviolet black light. Direct incandescent lights were banned outside the Gayway so as to make the island look softer and a bit more surreal than the usual street lighting guests were used to. More than 10,000 carefully concealed floodlights were needed to achieve the desired effects.

There were numerous other details taken into account, such as using mostly white lights on the facades on the western side of the island to make them more visible from the city, or suppressing light levels on the causeway from Yerba Buena Island to make the fair look like a magical island cut off from the rest of the world.

Magnificent as they were during the day, the fair buildings took on a whole new level of excitement at night. The buildings were not simply just lit; a massive amount of lighting was used to make them jump brightly out of the night sky. Here, one of the Elephant Towers glistens unlike any other building a visitor was likely to have ever seen elsewhere.

There were no bare light bulbs on the grounds other than in the Gayway. Even the street lighting had been specially planned, with a wide variety of lighting fixtures that were unique to the fair. Here, a row of lights softly illuminates the adjacent walkway without detracting from the glowing walls of the Tower Compound in the background.

The lighting systems had to throw beams of light to the highest reaches of buildings without blinding anyone at ground level. In some cases, such as seen here at the Mission Trails Building, lights concealed in the structures themselves gave a needed assist to the lighting on the ground.

Balancing all of the lights in an area was a task that took considerable calculation and planning and, at times, some adjustments after the initial results were seen. The spotlights pictured here behind the Tower of the Sun had to be strong enough to make a bold statement on their own, yet not overpower the lighting of the tower or the adjacent courts. The frequent San Francisco fog also added to the complexity of the task.

The lighting had to be done in such a way as to not call attention to itself, instead directing the eye toward the intended target. While rows of submerged lights can be seen in this view, the immediate attention was on the arching fountains. Diffused lenses helped soften lights in such situations, with colored filters employed as necessary.

The gold pillars at the entrance to the Court of the Great Seal, which was situated between the California and San Francisco buildings, took on a special glow when awash in light at night. The slender columns were illuminated by hidden lights in their bases and a ring of spotlights that encircled the roof. Benches throughout the area made it a perfect spot to relax while gazing at the Lakes of the Nations.

This view across the Lakes of the Nations toward Pacific House illustrates how the designers had worked carefully to craft a nighttime ambience of great visual appeal. Rather than bathing the exterior in bright lights, Pacific House stood out in the night sky due to the interior lighting pouring out of its great windows, highlighted by the spotlights behind its darkened silhouette. The reflections on the tranquil waters completed the effect.

This view of the Fountain of Life shows how well the lighting designers were able to achieve their goals. The statue and the column are lit well enough to showcase their details but done so without overpowering the fountains below. The Temple Compound in the rear is bright enough to be clearly seen—all without any distraction from the lights themselves.

The towering pagoda shone at night like a lighthouse, attracting late-staying visitors to the Gayway. While most of the site was softly illuminated with indirect lighting, the Gayway was full of neon and floodlights. The roller coaster and twin Ferris wheels can be seen brightly lit off to the left.

Once inside the Gayway there was plenty going on at night. The advertising was certainly not subdued, with shops brightly lit to entice passersby in for a game of chance, a quick spin on a ride, perhaps a piece of pie, or—for those too shy to enter in the light of day—a visit to one of the girlie shows. (Courtesy of Vince Bravo.)

Six

AFTER THE FAIR

When the gates swung shut on the GGIE for the last time on September 29, 1940, work quickly began on demolishing the fanciful structures that covered the grounds. The sound of bulldozers and wrecking balls replaced the happier sounds of the 17 million guests who had enjoyed the two seasons on Treasure Island.

All of this had been part of the original plans for the site, of course, but what happened next was a major change of direction that would forever alter the use of the man-made island. World War II was fast approaching, and with the loss of most air travel to the already conflict-stricken Far East, there was little incentive to complete the planned airport facilities, and all work on those plans was abandoned. As history would show, the development of longer-range land-based aircraft would have made Treasure Island and its seaplane facilities quickly obsolete in any event.

Instead, in early 1941, Treasure Island was leased to the US Navy for use as a training facility. The attack on Pearl Harbor led to a greater need for Navy facilities on the West Coast, and in April 1942, the Navy purchased the island, despite protests from the city that the price was far too low. Renamed Naval Station Treasure Island, the facility served the Navy in a wide variety of roles until it was finally decommissioned in 1996.

The City of San Francisco has been working on a master plan for the site ever since then—and is still arguing with the US government over pricing for the land. A visit today shows a rather motley collection of rundown ex-Navy buildings, storage yards of outdated fire trucks and other city vehicles, a splash of new development that includes attractive housing and retail shops, and a few remnants of the GGIE. The terminal buildings and the two massive hangars are tangible remnants of the Pageant of the Pacific and a must-visit for world's fair fans.

The long-term plans for Treasure Island remain incomplete as of this writing. The island is reportedly sinking 10 mm a year; hopefully, steps will be taken to address this while there is still time to preserve its amazing world's fair legacy.

This wartime shot of Treasure Island shows how the winds of war had swept most signs of the GGIE away. A few of the fair buildings were still in use, but this section of the island had been completely converted into a massive military hospital that provided acute care to more than 1,300 patients. A major care facility for the Pacific theater, the hospital was earmarked for closure in 1947, and the temporary buildings were later removed.

By 1957, most of the wartime buildings were gone as well as the last temporary structures from the fair. The base was serving as a training facility for a wide variety of naval skills and was quite an active facility. Simulated radiation cleanups were done on vessels such as the one docked here, with the unfortunate side effect that portions of the island are now awaiting cleanup for contaminated soil.

Visiting Treasure Island during the Navy years must have been a surreal experience at times. Here, sailor Ralph Quinn, based on the island for electronics training, gazes out at the remnants of the Fountain of Western Waters in 1950. Without any signage or other explanation of why it was there, the fountain looked quite out of place on a military installation. The fountain has since been removed and is in storage awaiting restoration. (Courtesy of Ralph Quinn.)

Here, Quinn poses with Brents Carlton's statue of a Polynesian woman. The Navy was unable to explain why this particular group of statues was left intact when the rest of the exposition was removed from Treasure Island. Happily, for whatever reason, it did survive—an amazing feat for something intended to last less than a year. (Courtesy of Ralph Quinn.)

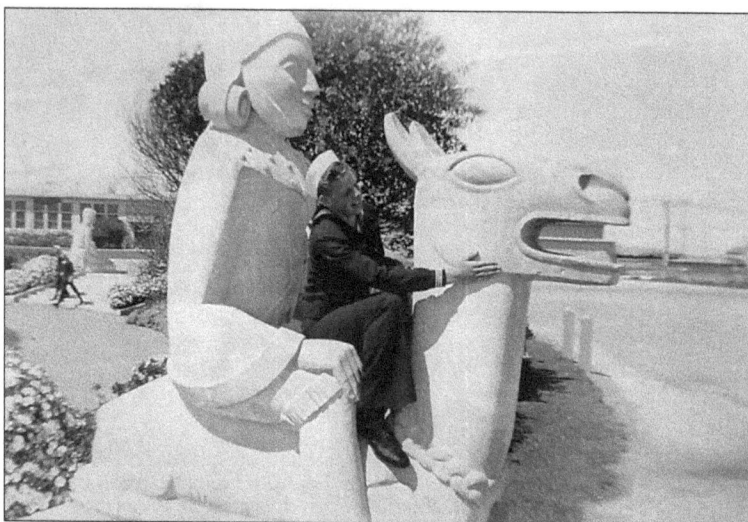

One of Sargent Johnson's llama figures was still extant, and sitting on it proved irresistible to Quinn. All of the statues appear to be in remarkably good shape given that they had been left to sit without care for more than a decade by this time. (Courtesy of Ralph Quinn.)

In 1973, Ralph Quinn took his family to Treasure Island to see his old Navy base. History has a way of repeating itself, and here Andrea, David, and Paul Quinn do their best to imitate their dad. The tree in the background sure grew in the intervening years! (Courtesy of Ralph Quinn.)

Movie magic was used to make it look like the actors were boarding a flying boat at Treasure Island in the 1981 blockbuster film *Raiders of the Lost Ark*. The plane was not seaworthy, so it had to be filmed on dry land. Matte paintings and camera angles were used to create the illusion that the plane would soon be departing with Indy and his partner.

Even more of Treasure Island was seen in 1989 in *Indiana Jones and the Last Crusade* when the administration building became the Berlin airport. The site was still an active-use Navy facility at the time, and the film crew was not allowed to place any Nazi symbols on the structure; they were added digitally in post-production, as was the larger control tower seen here.

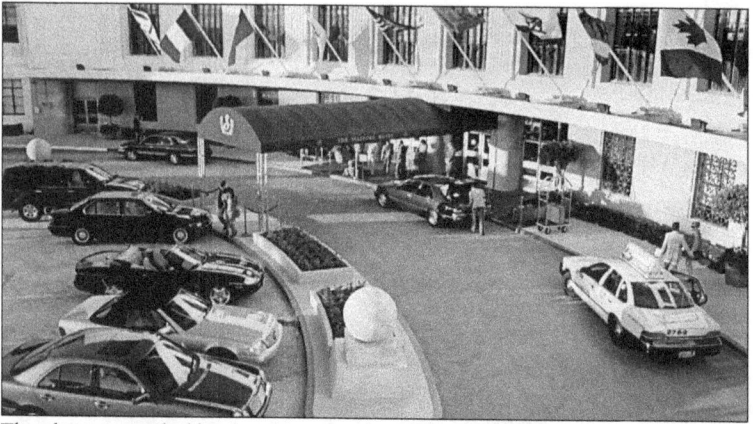

The administration building has also appeared in Hollywood productions in non-airport roles. In the 1998 version of *The Parent Trap* it was dressed up as the fictitious Stafford Hotel in San Francisco. A new entrance driveway, a canopy, and a row of flags helped complete the illusion, with careful camera angles masking the control tower on the roof.

Today, the site's administration building still looks exactly as originally intended—an airport terminal. The original control tower still sits atop the structure but is not used for any purposes other than occasional film shoots. Pieces of surviving statuary from the GGIE dot the walkway in front of the building.

The Spirit of India, Female by Jacques Schnier is one of the few surviving pieces of statuary from the GGIE and is on display now outside the administration building. It was one of 20 Pacific Unity figures that once graced the Court of Pacifica. Schnier also crafted aircraft-themed pieces at the ends of the airport terminal-turned-administration building.

Moving clockwise along the front of the building, a piece by Adaline Kent shows a young girl listening to music. It was part of three statues of that comprised the *Islands of the Pacific* among the Pacific unity figures. All of these statues are made of poured concrete with metal reinforcement rods.

Blowing a Horn (from a group called *Chinese Musicians*) is one of the two surviving pieces by Helen Phillips. All of these statues were left behind when the rest of the fair was demolished, but the Fountain of Western Waters was retained, at least for several years.

Next in line is *The Spirit of India, Male* by Jacques Schnier. During the 1940s, the Navy demolished the Fountain of Western Waters and replaced it with the Pacific Basin Fountain, a ceramic work shown during the fair at Pacific House. Amazingly, that fountain and these statues survived in the middle of a busy Navy base until the early 1990s.

The second of the remaining pieces by Adaline Kent is next. In 1994, the statues were moved to their current home and restored by the Treasure Island Museum Association. The Pacific Basin Fountain was cut into sections and placed in storage. Hopefully, funding can be secured so the statues can be placed in an appropriate setting in the future.

The Flutist by Helen Phillips is the last one on display. Ten more statues from the original group of 20 are in storage and awaiting restoration. Sadly, four appear to have been lost, with no records of their disposition.

The Treasure Island Museum is located inside the administration building but has been closed in recent years while the facility is being redeveloped. Staff is currently offering rotating exhibits and walking tours of the island during the development of a new permanent museum. A portion of the author's proceeds from this book will be donated to support their efforts.

The two hangars originally built for the planned airport are both still on the site. After the fair, they housed numerous Navy training facilities and simulators, but without the planned airport were generally not used for aircraft. Since the Navy pulled out, they have been used for a wide variety of purposes, including as soundstages for many television shows and movies.

The Spirit of Aerial Transportation by Carlo Taliabue may be showing a bit of wear, but this relief sculpture has been out in the ocean air now for more than 80 years. During the GGIE, it stood over the main entrance to the Hall of Transportation. All vestiges of the Pan Am signage that originally appeared under the sculpture are gone, like the airline itself.

A marker left from the Navy era commemorates the hangar's original dedication on October 26, 1938. While much of the fair footprint has been erased from the island over the years, the remaining structures provide a meaningful connection back to the two wonderful seasons of the Golden Gate International Exposition.

Visit us at
arcadiapublishing.com

www.ingramcontent.com/pod-product-compliance
Lightning Source LLC
Chambersburg PA
CBHW070335100426
42812CB00005B/1339